IRAN

Vijeya Rajendra & Gisela Kaplan & Rudi Rajendra

 Marshall Cavendish
Benchmark
New York

Humber College Library

PRECEDING PAGE
An Iranian man and boy with traditional musical instruments. The man is holding a four-stringed fiddle called a *kamen-chay* (kah-men-CHAY). It is made of wood and animal skin and is played vertically.

Marshall Cavendish Benchmark
99 White Plains Road
Tarrytown, NY 10591
Website: www.marshallcavendish.us

© Marshall Cavendish International (Asia) Private Limited 2004, 2006
© Times Media Private Limited 1993, 2003
All rights reserved. First edition 1993. Second edition 2003.
® "Cultures of the World" is a registered trademark of Times Publishing Limited.

Originated and designed by Times Editions
An imprint of Marshall Cavendish International (Asia) Private Limited
A member of the Times Publishing Limited

Library of Congress Cataloging-in-Publication Data
Rajendra, Vijeya, 1936-
Iran / by Vijeya Rajendra and Gisela Kaplan.— 2nd ed.
    p. cm. — (Cultures of the world)
Summary: Explores the geography, history, government, economy, people, and culture of Iran.
Includes bibliographical references and index.
    ISBN 0-7614-1665-X
    ISBN 9780-7614-1665-4
1. Iran—Juvenile literature. [1. Iran.] I. Kaplan, Gisela T. II.
Title. III. Series: Cultures of the world.
DS254.75.R353 2003
955—dc21   2003008257

Printed in China

7 6 5 4 3

CONTENTS

A detail of a bas-relief in Persepolis shows ambassadors from Syria and Lydia paying tribute to the Persian king Darius the Great. When Iran was Persia, its kings ruled over much of the Middle East and parts of Africa, Europe, and Central Asia.

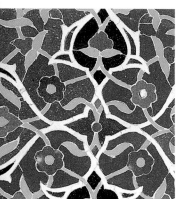

Decorations in a mosque. Islam renewed a fading Persian culture by bringing Arab patronage to Persian art, riches from distant lands, and new knowledge from scientific discoveries.

INTRODUCTION

IRAN'S NAME COMES FROM the word Aryan, meaning "noble." The Land of the Aryans was for centuries called Persia by outsiders. The Persian kings ruled one of the world's greatest empires—it covered most of western and southwestern Asia and parts of Africa and Europe. Iranians today have retained the language of their ancestors—they speak modern Persian, also known as Farsi.

Iran is an Islamic republic—the country is ruled by a class of religious leaders. Islam was introduced in Iran by the early Arabs, and most Iranians today practice a version of Islam called Shiism.

GEOGRAPHY

LOCATED IN SOUTHWESTERN ASIA, Iran shares borders with several countries and bodies of water: Iraq and Turkey in the west; Armenia, Azerbaijan, the Caspian Sea, and Turkmenistan in the north; Afghanistan and Pakistan in the east; and the Persian Gulf and the Gulf of Oman in the south.

Iran is more than twice the size of Texas in the United States and is more densely populated than many other oil-producing nations in the Middle East. More than 66 million people live in an area of 636,296 square miles (1,648,000 square km), much of which is desert.

For hundreds of years, overland trade routes crossed northern Iran, exposing it to many cultures. Iran's strategic position between Asia and Europe has attracted the attention of powers such as Great Britain and Russia in the past when empire building was at a peak. These powerful neighbors gradually eroded its frontiers in the 19th century, leaving only a shadow of the great country Iran once was.

Left: **Camels carry the belongings of nomads across rocky Iranian terrain under a cloudless blue sky.**

Opposite: **A section of the plateau landscape in Iran.**

7

LAND OF MOUNTAINS

A combination of volcanic cones, jagged mountains, lofty peaks, and barren deserts makes for a unique landscape. Iran's tallest mountain is Damavand, with a snow-covered peak all year round. So majestic in appearance is Damavand that early Iranians told tales of heroes and demons who lived on the mountain. Other volcanoes in Iran include the 12,162-foot-tall (3,707-m-tall) Sahand and the 12,805-foot-tall (3,903-m-tall) Lesser Ararat.

Located in a major seismic belt, Iran has suffered many devastating earthquakes. The country is blessed with natural resources, including petroleum and natural gas.

A snow-covered volcano in Iran.

Copper is one of the most important minerals in Iran. Two of the country's largest copper mines are Miduk and Sarcheshmeh, both in the province of Kermanshah. Iran's deserts have plentiful supplies of salt. Other minerals found in Iran include asbestos, chromium, gold, iron ore, lead, manganese, sulfur, tungsten, turquoise, uranium, and zinc.

Rising around 3,000 to 5,000 feet (914 to 1,524 m) above sea level, the Iranian plateau dominates much of the country's interior. The Iranian plateau is almost surrounded by mountain ranges—to the west lie the Zagros Mountains, Iran's longest range, while to the north lie the Elburz Mountains, including the highest peak in the country.

RIVERS

Iran's main navigable river is the 450-mile-long (724-km-long) Karun. Its source is in the Zagros Mountains. The Karun river empties into the Persian Gulf through the 120-mile-long (193-km-long) Shatt al-Arab, a tidal river formed by the confluence of the Euphrates and Tigris rivers. The Shatt al-Arab forms part of the border between Iran and Iraq.

There are four main drainage basins in Iran: the Caspian Sea; the Persian Gulf; the two great deserts, Dasht-e Kavir and Dasht-e Lut; and the largest lake completely within Iran, Daryacheh-ye Orumiyeh. In winter streams bring water to the deserts and form salt lakes, but these dry up in summer.

Sparkling rivers and lush forests and meadows in the Elburz Mountains, whose slopes catch rain from clouds that blow in from the Caspian Sea.

A hill and lake scene in Pol-e Dokhtar, Lorestan.

SCARCITY OF WATER

Salt lakes are a prominent feature of the Iranian desert landscape. There are two kinds of salt lakes: a *kavir* (KEH-veer) is an often dangerous salt marsh, while a *namak* (NAH-mahk) is usually shallow and has less mud. The salt in these lakes shines with a blinding brightness in the harsh Iranian sun.

The Kavir Buzurg, or Great Kavir, and other salt lakes in the Dasht-e Kavir have characteristics similar to quicksand, making the desert dangerous terrain for inexperienced travelers.

Freshwater lakes are rare in Iran. To bring water to drier areas, early Iranians developed a clever system of irrigation. By building a long tunnel called a *qanat* (kah-NUT) deep in the ground, they could transport underground water to a dry area. A network of such tunnels made it possible to cultivate land that was previously too dry to farm. *Qanat* networks are also used to channel water from the valleys to the villages and fields. The *qanat* method is still used to irrigate desert land not only in Iran, but also in other Middle Eastern nations such as Oman.

Another solution to the scarcity of water in Iran is the construction of dams. This technique dates back to the time of the early Iranians—dikes hundreds of years old have been discovered in Khorasan province.

More recently, the Iranian government has built a number of large dams; the largest is the Karun III on the Karun river. The seventh largest dam in the world, the Karun III stands at a height of 673 feet (205 m). Besides providing water for irrigation, dams also supply water and generate electricity for the cities.

Leaves rustle in the breeze by the Caspian Sea.

CLIMATE

Iran is a land of extreme climates, with hot summers and cold winters in most parts of the country. Days can get very hot, while night temperatures can plunge. Iran's sheltered location in a vast landmass and its encircling mountain ranges shut out the moderating influence of the ocean.

Most of Iran's rainfall occurs during the winter months, between November and April, and rains are usually light showers. Iran's most watered parts are in the north and west. The Caspian Sea coast is the only place where there is sufficient rainfall to farm without irrigation. The rest of the country receives very little rain annually: about 12 inches (30.5 cm) in the Iranian plateau and 5 inches (12.7 cm) in the desert lands covering most of the country. The skies over Iran are usually clear and cloudless for lack of moisture.

Temperatures in Tehran range from 27°F to 45°F (-2.8°C to 7.2°C) in January, the coldest month, and from 72°F to 99°F (22.2°C to 37.2°C) in July, the hottest month. Frost is common during winter, and snow covers the mountain peaks most of the year. Melting snow is another source of water for agriculture and personal consumption.

IRANIAN FLORA

Iran's vegetation reflects the country's climate and its position between Asia and Africa. Shrubs and thorn plants are common in Iran, where 75 percent of the land is arid or semi-arid. Many of these shrubs are either spiny or prickly to reduce the loss of moisture. In the salt regions, plants are resistant to both salt and drought.

Iranian shrubs produce a variety of useful substances, such as gum, licorice, and camel's thorn, which yields Persian manna. Poppy, sesame, tamarind, and tarragon lend flavor to food, while henna, indigo, and saffron are traditional coloring agents.

A wide range of herbs thrives at higher elevations. The slopes of the Zagros consist mainly of grasslands and woodlands, and wildflowers bloom in spring. Wildflowers in Iran include buttercups, geraniums, gladioli, irises, orchids, and roses, the country's most popular flower, beautifully represented in paintings and carpet designs.

The Caspian and Zagros forests are populated by shrubs, ferns, and trees such as elm, maple, oak, walnut, pear, plum, and pistachio. (The export of pistachio nuts is an important contributor to Iran's economy.) Juniper, almond, and fruit trees grow in the plateau area, while the oases support date palms and acacia, poplar, and willow trees.

IRANIAN FAUNA

Iran is home to a wide variety of wild animals. Zagros mountain fauna include brown and black bears, foxes, Persian squirrels, and gazelles. Caspian forest fauna include red and roe deer, wild pigs, and tigers. Panthers still roam many areas of Iran, and there are small populations of cheetahs and leopards. Other wild animals include hedgehogs, hyenas, ibex, jackals, rabbits, wolves, and wild asses, goats, pigs, and sheep.

Iranian sheep graze in green pastures sheltered by mountains.

Species of birds found in Iran include eagles, partridges, pelicans, pheasants, shrikes, sparrows, and vultures. Ducks, geese, and seagulls populate the coastal areas in the north and south of the country. Other birds living in or passing through Iran include flamingoes, kingfishers, nightjars, swallows, swans, and woodpeckers.

Iran has a variety of marine life, with around 200 species of fish. Lobsters and turtles live in the Persian Gulf, while beluga and Iranian sturgeon swim in the Caspian Sea. (Sturgeon eggs, or caviar, are an important source of export revenue for Iran.) Otters swim the rivers of the Zagros Mountains, and trout live in abundance in the mountain streams. Iran's waterways also support large populations of herring, mullet, salmon, and tuna.

13

HISTORY

EVIDENCE OF WIDESPREAD human settlement in Iran dates back to the seventh or sixth millennium B.C., when village farmers populated the Iranian plateau and the Khuzestan lowlands. Elamites appeared in the fourth millennium B.C. in the Khuzestan lowlands, and Indo-European Iranians became prominent on the plateau during the Iron Age.

By the ninth century B.C., two major groups of Iranians appeared: the Medes and the Persians. In the early sixth century B.C., the Medes allied with the Babylonians, Egyptians, and Lydians to rule a vast part of the Middle East, including Iran.

However, in 550 B.C., Cyrus the Great led the Persians in battle and defeated the Medes. He founded the Achaemenid (AH-KAY-me-nid) empire, and the conquered Medes also became known as Persians.

Left: **A bas-relief depicting life in the court of Darius the Great.**

Opposite: **The Gate of All Nations at Persepolis, the capital of the Achaemenid empire, which stretched from Libya and Egypt in Africa to Thrace and Macedonia in the Mediterranean and east to the Indus River in India.**

THE ACHAEMENID EMPIRE

By 539 B.C., Cyrus had conquered vast areas of land, including Babylonia, Palestine, Syria, and Asia Minor. (The Bible mentions Cyrus as the liberator of Jews who had been held captive in Babylon.)

Cyrus was also noted for his humane policies. For example, he allowed his conquered subjects to keep their own religion. In fact, the Persians adopted much from the culture of the lands they controlled, including Iran, and this greatly enriched Persian culture. The Persians constructed magnificent buildings and good roads and even established shipping lines.

Darius and Xerxes (ZERK-ses) were other well-known kings who further expanded the Achaemenid empire, creating the largest empire of the time. Persian soldiers were excellent archers. In war, ranks of bowmen would shoot hundreds of arrows at the enemy from a long distance, thus overwhelming the enemy before hand-to-hand fighting began.

However, the Persians were unable to defeat the Greeks. The Persians were driven back by the numerically inferior Greeks at Marathon in 490 B.C. and Salamis in 480 B.C. The Achaemenid empire came to an end with the conquest of Persepolis by Alexander the Great in 330 B.C.

Only 20 years old when he became king of Macedonia, Alexander set out to conquer the world with great enthusiasm and won nearly all his battles. He introduced Greek culture and political structure in Persian lands, and many Greek soldiers settled there. Alexander respected the Persian aristocracy and chose young Persians to train for his army. He sought to unite the Persians and the Greeks through intermarriage. He

Above: **A vestige of ancient Persepolis.**

Opposite: **The tomb of Darius the Great.**

p18: **Sassanian relief sculpture at Nacht-e Rostam.**

p19: **A symbol of Iran's Islamic heritage.**

married a Persian princess, Roxana of Sogdiana, and encouraged his generals to marry Persian nobles' daughters.

Alexander died in 323 B.C. at the age of 32. He left no heir to his vast empire, and his generals fought for control. One of them, Seleucus, finally won, and he founded the Seleucid dynasty.

But unlike Alexander, the Seleucids were not popular among the Iranian nobility. They also faced rebellions by the nomads, who fought with the settled people.

THE PARTHIAN KINGDOM

Migration of Iranian peoples such as the Yüeh-chih and the Parni contributed to the decline of Seleucid rule in Iran. Parni nomads from northern Iran invaded the Seleucid province of Parthia southeast of the Caspian Sea. They established an indigenous Parthian kingdom, with their chief, Arsaces, as king, in about 250 B.C.

Future Parthian rulers extended their kingdom to include lands from Armenia to present-day Pakistan. Parthian rule lasted around 500 years, until a new Persian dynasty arose.

THE SASSANIAN DYNASTY

In A.D. 224 Ardashir I, ruler of a Persian state in the province of Fars, declared war against the Parthian king Artabanus V. Ardashir defeated Artabanus, ending the Arsacid dynasty of the Parthians and founding the Sassanian dynasty of the Persians.

The Sassanids established Zoroastrianism as the official state religion and founded or rebuilt many cities and dug canals and built bridges. Architecture from the Sassanian era includes many Zoroastrian fire temples and the palace of Ardashir I in Fars province.

Ardashir, claiming the title "king of kings," actively expanded the empire and took the city of Ctesiphon in present-day Iraq as the capital. His son, Shapur I, and future Sassanid emperors continued to defend and expand the empire, even in the face of wars with the Romans. The Sassanids took back western lands once part of the Achaemenid empire.

In the early 600s King Khosrow II reached Chalcedon, near Constantinople (present-day Istanbul), the capital of the Byzantine empire. The Byzantine emperor Heraclius fought back and defeated Khosrow battle after battle, and the Persians gradually lost the territories they had conquered.

ARAB CONQUEST

Weakened by wars, the Sassanids and much of the Byzantine empire fell to the Arabs in their explosive expansion out of the Arabian peninsula after the founding of the Islamic state there.

To the lands they conquered, the Arabs brought a new religion, Islam. Over time, most Persians embraced Islam. The Arabs also brought a new language, Arabic. Many Arabic words entered the Persian language, and modern Persian uses Arabic script.

The Abbasid period remained for nearly 600 years. During this period, famous Persians such as poet Omar Khayyam brought glory to the Persian civilization. Persian culture became popular and widespread. Europeans began to study Persian science and appreciate Persian arts—literature, music, painting, and carpets.

Arab control weakened during the 900s, and Iran was broken into a number of small kingdoms. Several Turkish military groups took control from A.D. 1000 until the Mongols attacked in 1220.

A tomb left by one of the many invaders of Iran.

MONGOL ATTACKS

Under the leadership of Genghis Khan, the Mongols sacked Iran's cities and massacred many inhabitants. The greatest of Iran's cities was Baghdad, which the Abbasids founded on the Tigris in A.D. 762. Baghdad was for centuries the center of rule in the Middle East. In 1258 Baghdad was destroyed by the Mongols, and it never fully recovered.

Genghis Khan's grandson, Hülegü, founded the Il-Khanid dynasty and made Tabriz the capital. The Il Khans ruled a vast territory that included Iran, Iraq, the Caucasus, and parts of Asia Minor.

After 1335 the Il-Khanid empire broke into several minor dynasties. Timur (also known as Tamerlane), a descendant of Genghis Khan, attempted to establish Mongol rule again, but he never managed to unify his empire.

THE SAFAVID DYNASTY

In 1501 the Persians regained power in the Middle East through the Safavids, a Turkish people. The most famous Safavid ruler was Shah Abbas I (1588–1629), under whose rule Iran prospered.

Shah Abbas the Great centralized administration at the new capital, Esfahan. He reorganized the Persian army and made alliances with the Europeans against the Ottomans. With his army, Shah Abbas resisted the Ottoman invaders and tribal raiders. However, his greatest achievements were in the arts.

Persian architecture reached new heights of beauty under the shah's patronage. He built the magnificent city of Esfahan, which gave rise to the saying *"Esphahan nesf-e-jehan"* (ES-FAH-hahn nesf-je-hahn), meaning "Esfahan is half of the world." Travelers to Persia from the court of England's Queen Elizabeth I went back home with glowing accounts of Persia's splendor.

The Safavid dynasty fell when Afghans invaded Iran and captured Esfahan in 1722. However, the Afghan interlude was short-lived.

A Turk, Nader Shah (1736–47), assembled his own navy and built a large army. Nader Shah not only drove out the Afghans and reunited Iran, but later went on to conquer Afghanistan itself. Faced with a lack of money, Nader Shah decided to invade Delhi in India and bring to Iran the Mughal emperor's precious stones and jewelry. The loot helped Nader Shah to finance his empire, without imposing taxes in Iran.

In 1747 Nader Shah was assassinated, and his army fell apart, with commanders aiming to set up their own states. Civil war between rival factions—the Zands and the Qajars—followed.

The royal city of Esfahan is over 500 years old. It teems with monuments of Safavid art.

Qajar tilework in the Golestan Palace depicts the Persian symbol of a sun rising behind a lion.

THE QAJAR DYNASTY

The Qajar leader Agha Muhammad Khan led an army to overthrow the Zands and conquer Iran. He became the first king of the Qajar dynasty in 1796 but was murdered soon after. In 1797 his nephew Fath 'Ali Shah ascended the throne.

During the 19th century, Iran was reluctantly involved in the political quarrels and colonial intrigues of Europe. Iran's strategic location was part of the problem. It lay between two warring nations: Great Britain and Russia. Russia, whose ports were frozen in winter and spring, was anxious to gain entry to the warm waters of the Caspian Sea, while Great Britain was on alert for any threat to the most important part of its empire—India.

The Qajar rulers needed revenue badly and granted concessions to Russia and Great Britain in return for loans. The conditions of the loans gave these two powers a lot of control over Iran's internal affairs, and they began to encroach into Iranian territory.

As a result, many Iranians came into contact with the Western world during the Qajar era. Europeans came to Iran to construct modern infrastructure. Their presence was controversial, because they did not always respect local traditions or values. But this exposure to Western ideas also introduced the concept of political freedom to Iran, and in 1906 the shah was forced to proclaim a constitution.

During World War I, despite appeals for respect for its neutrality, Iran was occupied by British and Russian troops. In 1921 an Iranian officer, Reza Khan, took control of the Iranian military, and in 1925 he deposed the last Qajar king. In 1926 Reza Khan founded the Pahlavi dynasty.

THE PAHLAVI DYNASTY

Reza Shah Pahlavi set out to modernize and Westernize Iran through many reforms. He introduced civil law, established the first national bank, modified divorce law in favor of women (who were no longer permitted to wear a veil), and sought independence from foreign interference. The name of the country was officially changed from Persia to Iran in 1935.

During World War II, owing to Iran's ties with Nazi Germany and its policy of neutrality, the shah refused to expel Germans from Iran and denied Allied forces passage through Iran. Needing to transport U.S. war supplies to the Soviet Union through Iran, British and Soviet forces invaded Iran in 1941, forcing the shah to leave. He was succeeded by his son, Muhammad Reza.

Faced with the task of restoring the country, the new shah set out to redistribute land, reduce illiteracy, and build industry. However, opposition to his pro-Western rule grew intense, as people organized anti-shah groups and wrote articles attacking government corruption and the shah's excessive lifestyle. At the same time, a movement was growing to end British control of the oil industry. This movement was led by Muhammad Mossadeq. Britain responded by boycotting Iranian oil. This and other factors led to severe financial losses in Iran. Mossadeq and his followers forced the shah into exile. But the shah, with help from the United States, returned after a few days, and Mossadeq was arrested. In 1978 Iranians held massive demonstrations, which forced the shah to flee his country the following year. He died in exile in 1980.

The founder of the Pahlavi dynasty, Reza Shah.

Muhammad Reza, Iran's last shah.

AN ISLAMIC REPUBLIC

During Muhammad Reza Shah's reign, Iran became increasingly Westernized, but many Iranians considered this transformation an insult to the traditional values of Islam. Rapid industrialization also meant ballooning populations in the cities, resulting in social problems.

The angry Iranian people gave their support to Ayatollah Ruhollah Khomeini, a religious leader in exile since his arrest in 1963. Widespread civil unrest brought down Iran's monarchy in January 1979.

Ayatollah Khomeini then returned to Iran and proclaimed it an Islamic republic. He declared an end to Western influences in Iran, and those who broke the fundamentalist Islamic social codes were caught by patroling revolutionaries and severely punished. Many foreign-educated upper- and middle-class Iranians fled the country and settled overseas. The new regime also carried out a brutal campaign to eliminate opponents.

In November 1979, after the exiled shah went to the United States for cancer treatment, the Ayatollah's supporters took more than 60 Americans hostage at the U.S. embassy in Tehran. The hostages were not freed until January 1981.

WAR WITH IRAQ

Border disputes, such as that over the Shatt al-Arab front, have long been a source of tension between Iran and Iraq. In 1980 an old border dispute erupted into a war that lasted eight years and resulted in great loss of life and resources on both sides.

As internal political problems weakened Iran, Saddam Hussein's Iraqi regime saw a chance to attack, and tried to seize Iran's oil-producing province of Khuzestan. The Iranian army put up a surprising defense, and throughout the war both sides suffered massive losses, especially in population centers and at oil refineries. The Iran-Iraq war ended in 1988, with a UN resolution for a mutual ceasefire.

In 1989 another tragedy struck Iran when Ayatollah Khomeini died of a heart attack. Even as the nation mourned Khomeini's death, Iran's president, Ali Khamenei, was given the title of *ayatollah*, or sign of god. A new president, Hashemi Rafsanjani, was then elected.

A great revolution is never the fault of the people but of the government.

—Goethe

A mass funeral at the Mehrabad airport in Tehran in 2002 for Iranian soldiers who died in Iraq during the war.

President Syed Muhammad Khatami makes a speech in Shiraz in 2001.

MENDING DIPLOMATIC TIES

Hashemi Rafsanjani's presidency marked the start of a more progressive and pragmatic era in Iran's recent history, especially in trade and foreign policy. In 1990 Iran resumed relations with the United Kingdom. This paved the way toward mending ties with the West, which would bring foreign investment sorely needed to rebuild the wartorn nation.

In the 1990s a major problem in relations with the West was global terrorism. In 1995 the United States imposed a ban on trade with Iran for having allegedly sponsored terrorist groups in the Middle East.

Iran's fifth president raised hopes of radical reforms in the country and renewed relations with the West. Elected in 1997, President Syed Muhammad Khatami examined ideas such as democracy and set the nation on the path of social and political change. While this generated opposition from the conservatives, the West found the pace of reform too slow.

Relations with much of the West, in particular the United States, remained volatile at the beginning of the 21st century. President Khatami continued efforts to develop dialogue with the United States—something that Ayatollah Khamenei remained strongly opposed to. In 2001 Iran condemned the World Trade Center terror attacks and helped to establish a post-Taliban government in Afghanistan, but it did not support the U.S. military campaign. In 2002 the United States accused Iran of being part of an "axis of evil" that harbors terrorists and weapons of mass destruction.

IRANGATE

Irangate was the name given to a political scandal in the United States involving the secret sale of weapons to Iran in 1985, violating U.S. government policy. At a time when the United States was calling for a worldwide ban on sending arms to Iran, it had used profits from a secret trade in arms with Iran to help the contra guerrillas in Nicaragua. The arms were believed to have been sold to Iran via Israel.

Iranian protesters march with an effigy of then U.S. President Ronald Reagan in a wave of anti-U.S. hysteria. The Iranians blamed the United States for anti-Islamic culture in Iran.

GOVERNMENT

IRAN IS GOVERNED based on the constitution that was approved in a national referendum following the revolution in 1979. A national referendum in 1989 approved amendments to the constitution of 1979.

Iran's constitution is unique. It is based on a new concept—Islamic government—created by Ayatollah Khomeini. This system of government rules according to God's law first, and then the law of men.

The supreme leader, the *vali-ye faqih* (VAH-li-yee fah-kee), is considered to be the representative of the Twelfth Imam according to Shi'a doctrine. The *faqih* is elected for life by an Assembly of Experts—a committee of 86 theologians who are publicly elected to an eight-year term. The *faqih* is respected for his theological knowledge and has final authority in all decisions made by the executive, legislative, and judicial branches. The *faqih* can veto any legislation passed by the executive branch. The current *faqih* is Ayatollah Seyed Ali Khamenei.

Above: **Iranian president Khatami addresses the sixth Economic Cooperation Organization (ECO) summit in Tehran in 2000.**

Opposite: **The Azadi (Freedom) monument in Tehran.**

THE PRESIDENT

The executive branch of the Iranian government consists of a Council of Ministers headed by a president. Before 1989 the executive branch included a prime minister, who chose the members of the cabinet and led executive duties, while the president filled a largely ceremonial position.

Constitutional amendments in 1989 removed the prime minister and expanded the role of the president. The president is now the head of government and is elected to a four-year term. President Khatami was reelected in 2001.

The Senate in Tehran. The Majlis meets here to debate and legislate.

LAWS AND COURTS

A unicameral Islamic Consultative Assembly called the Majlis (MAHJ-lis) drafts legislation. The 290 members of the Majlis are publicly elected for a four-year term.

A conservative Council of Guardians reviews any legislation passed by the Majlis to ensure that it follows Shar'iah, or Islamic, law. The council is made up of 12 jurists—six are chosen by the *faqih*, and six are recommended by the head of the judiciary and then appointed by the Majlis.

The Council of Guardians has the power to strike down and send back to the Majlis for revision any legislation it deems not in line with Islamic law or the constitution. When disputes arise between the Majlis and the Council of Guardians, the Expediency Council mediates. This council includes some of Iran's most powerful men, who are appointed by the *faqih*. The council's chairman is the former president, Rafsanjani.

The judicial branch of the Iranian government consists of the Supreme Court and a network of subordinate courts. Besides civil and criminal courts, there are special courts in Iran that hear charges of clerical misconduct or terrorism and national security offences.

LOCAL GOVERNMENT

At the local level, Iran is divided into 28 provinces, each divided into counties, and each county has several districts and subdistricts. The Ministry of the Interior appoints a governor to each province and each county and a mayor to each city.

DEFENSE

The commander-in-chief of Iran's armed forces is not the president, but the *faqih*. The *faqih* decides on all matters concerning national security and defense. The Supreme National Security Council organizes internal and external defense. The council includes the president, leaders of the armed forces and the Revolutionary Guard, and ministers in charge of foreign and internal affairs.

Iran's armed forces consist of the army and the Revolutionary Guard. The army protects the nation's territory against foreign intrusion or invasion; the Revolutionary Guard enforces Islamic law in daily life and monitors opponents to the regime. The Revolutionary Guard has also supported Islamic revolutionary movements in other countries.

ELECTIONS

Iran holds presidential and parliamentary elections every four years. Political parties include the Islamic Iran Participation Front (the largest reformist party, led by the brother of the president), the conservative Followers of the Imam's Line, and the Green Party, which campaigns for the natural environment and against the production of nuclear, chemical, and biological weapons.

Election candidates have to be Muslim Iranian citizens age 25 and above, and they must be loyal to the *faqih*. Election committees screen all applicants, but the Council of Guardians makes the final approval or rejection. Candidates can start campaigning only after the final list of approved applicants has been issued.

Iranians are eligible to vote for government leaders from age 15. Women and youth are a growing voice in the electorate.

Hashemi Rafsanjani was born in 1934 and studied under Ayatollah Khomeini. Elected president in 1989 (and reelected in 1993), Rafsanjani worked to revive a failing economy and mend ties with other countries. He also supported women's rights in higher education and paid employment.

POWER STRUGGLE

Deep rifts in the government are the main reason for Iran's slow, problematic reforms. Two camps are caught in a power struggle—the reformists led by President Khatami and the conservatives led by Ayatollah Khamenei.

With the reformists pushing for a more democratic Iran and the conservatives clinging to the strict codes of the revolution, strong differences in opinion as to how Iran should be governed continue to hinder social, economic, and political reforms that would improve the country's global image.

CENSORSHIP

For conservatives, the role of the mass media is to propagate Islamic culture and avoid propagating anti-Islamic culture. Publications have to be licensed, and the constitution guarantees press freedom. However, publications have been shut down and journalists jailed for printing articles deemed detrimental to Islam or the revolution.

Public support in the 2000 parliamentary elections for liberal parties such as the Freethinkers' Front alarmed conservatives, who began a crackdown on the press. They imprisoned activists, banned political parties, and suspended or closed publications.

Since 2000 many newspapers have been banned or suspended, including *Nourooz*, the Iranian Morning Daily, which moved onto the Internet, and the similarly named *Ruz-e Now*. Since 2000 also many pro-reformist journalists have been tried in the revolutionary courts and sentenced to serve jail terms. In 2001 the Iran Freedom Movement opposition party was banned on charges that it was trying to overthrow the establishment.

Many banned publications have found an alternative avenue—the Internet—to reach audiences. Media censorship has not yet caught up with media technology, and thousands of Iranians with access to the Internet are still able to read publications that the conservative authorities are trying to silence.

POLITICAL FIGURES

Several politicians and religious leaders have been central to the emergence and development of the Islamic Republic of Iran. In particular, Ayatollah Khomeini (*mural below*) was the first *vali-ye faqih*. Indeed the revolution that brought about the fall of the monarchy was called in his name.

Born in 1900, Khomeini was trained as a clergyman and in the 1930s became one of the leaders in the opposition to Reza Shah. In 1964 Khomeini was exiled from Iran and fled to Iraq. In 1978 he fled to France. While in exile, he organized the opposition to the shah that in 1979 led to the successful overthrow of the monarchy.

Khomeini succeeded in bringing about his vision of a new Islamic order, free from Western influence, due partly to his charisma and partly to the turn of the revolution, when many of his contemporaries shared his anti-Americanism, vividly expressed in posters and slogans. Despite misgivings among some of the clergy, Khomeini's plan to turn Iran into a strictly religious society was put in place. Khomeini became the unquestioned leader of Iran and stayed in power unchallenged until his death in 1989.

A much more recent though no less significant player in Iranian politics and government is Muhammad Khatami, whose father was a friend of Khomeini. Elected the country's fifth president in 1997 in a landslide victory with almost 70 percent of the popular vote, Khatami was reelected in 2001, with an even larger following (around 77 percent of the popular vote).

Born in 1943 in Ardakan in Yazd province, Khatami began studying theology in 1961 in Qom. He later went to universities in Esfahan and Tehran. He married Zohreh Sadeghi in 1974; they have three children. Khatami speaks several languages, including Arabic, German, and English.

President Khatami has a different public image from Iran's other leaders. He is a people's leader, who promises a more democratic future for Iran.

ECONOMY

THE IRANIAN ECONOMY expanded at a very fast pace in the second half of the 20th century. During this time the government built gigantic steel plants, oil refineries, and factories.

The Iran-Iraq war, which lasted through most of the 1980s, disrupted economic development in Iran. The war resulted in more than a million deaths in Iran and extensive damage to the country's natural environment and economic infrastructure. Iran's production of crude oil, an important revenue source, dipped drastically after bombing raids damaged oil fields.

Above: **Rural farmers harvest grain in the Azarbayjan districts.**

Opposite: **Iranians shop in the Esfahan bazaar.**

Signs of recovery began to show after the war. In the early 1990s Iran's crude oil production capacity surpassed 1,200 million barrels per year, from under 800 million toward the end of the war. By 2002 this figure was greater than 1,500 million barrels. Iran has the second-largest share of crude oil production in the Organization of the Petroleum Exporting Countries (OPEC).

Iran is also largely self-sufficient in food production for domestic consumption. Large-scale irrigation projects have made desert areas agriculturally productive and have significantly expanded the country's agricultural output.

However, the Iranian economy remains heavily repressed under government control. Political stability is a crucial factor in attempts to resolve the country's economic problems.

Sheep are the most numerous of Iran's livestock.

AGRICULTURE

Agriculture accounts for 20 percent of Iran's gross domestic product and engages 30 percent of the labor force. Only around 10 percent of Iran's land is arable. Most of the country's crops, including sugar beet, cotton, and wool, are cultivated near the Caspian Sea, north of Tehran. Grains, especially wheat and rice, are the most important crops, while pistachio nuts are another big earner, making up 10 percent of non-oil exports.

Livestock—sheep, goats, cattle, donkeys, horses, and camels—are used for their services in transportation and in plowing fields or for their hide or milk to make food and other products.

Access to the Caspian Sea and the Persian Gulf has led to the growth of an active fishing industry, particularly in caviar—sturgeon eggs.

An oil refinery in Abadan, a town in southern Iran. Situated near the Persian Gulf, this town is a major oil refining and export center.

HEAVY INDUSTRY

The Iranian economy depends heavily on the export of crude oil and natural gas, which account for more than 80 percent of export earnings. Iran's natural gas deposits are the second largest in the world; its oil reserves are the fifth largest.

Iran's oil fields are located mainly in the southwestern province of Khuzestan and in the Persian Gulf. The country also claims some of the reserves in the Caspian Sea. Most of Iran's gas reserves lie in the Persian Gulf, in the South Pars field, shared with Qatar. Oil and natural gas are transported through pipelines both domestically and into neighboring countries. One such pipeline runs for about 1,590 miles (2,559 km) from Tabriz in the north to Ankara in Turkey.

Iran's non-oil industries have been growing since the 1990s, as the government places increasing emphasis on reducing the country's dependence on oil and gas revenues. Iran's non-oil industries include, apart from agriculture, the extraction of minerals and metals and the manufacture of industrial goods such as automobiles and tractors. Most of these industries are located in Tehran province.

Above: **Carpets for sale in Shiraz are displayed even on the walls and overhead.**

Opposite: **A tile maker transforms a block of stone into decorative pieces for the wall.**

PERSIAN CARPETS

Persian carpet weaving has a very long history. For centuries, Persian rugs have been at the center of the home. People kneel on carpets to pray and sit to eat. Nomads placed carpets at the entrance to their tents and covered the ground inside the tent so that they could sit or sleep more comfortably. The oldest rug believed to be of Persian origin dates back to around 500 B.C. It was discovered in 1949 in the Siberian Altai region.

Authentic Persian carpets are handmade from natural fibers and are valued internationally for their beauty and quality, the result of a deep-rooted artisan tradition. There are many carpet-producing regions in Iran; two of the more famous Persian weaves come from the Hamadan region and Bijar in Kermanshah province. Iran exports most of its carpets to Europe, especially Germany.

HANDICRAFT PRODUCTION

Apart from its world-renowned carpets, Iran has several other handicraft traditions. Hamadan is known for its pottery, ceramics, and leather works. From Gorgan and Mashhad come bonnets, embroidered sheepskin coats, and dresses, tunics, and blouses made from natural silk, known as *kalaghe* (KAH-lah-gi). Bakhtaran, the largest city of western Iran, produces knitted footwear.

The Khorasan mine in Mashhad produces turquoise, which is worked into all kinds of jewelry. Timber is rare in Iran, and hence woodwork and wooden items are not high on the crafts list, but wooden carvings and wooden kitchen tools are sold around the Caucasian mountains and near the Caspian Sea. Pottery, ceramics, and glasswork, however, can be found throughout Iran, and pottery, especially, has experienced a recent revival and renaissance led by the National Crafts School in Tehran.

CARPET WEAVING

Carpet weaving is a specialized, laborious, and time-consuming art. It may take as long as a year or two to finish one carpet by the traditional method of a knotted stitch, done on a loom. There are mainly two kinds of knotted stitch: a Turkish knot, which involves the use of a needle; and a Persian knot, which is made without a needle and used for very fine carpets. One square yard of high-quality carpet may have up to a million knots, and an average carpet about 200,000. On average, a highly-skilled weaver can make about 12,000 knots a day.

When the weaving is finished, the carpet has to go through two more processes: the fibers are crushed to make the carpet pliable; and then the carpet is washed and dried. In some areas, such as the Rey neighborhood near Tehran, these processes have become a tourist attraction.

FOREIGN TRADE

The Islamic Revolution, war with Iraq, and trade sanctions have had devastating effects on the Iranian economy. In the last few decades the country's international debt has grown. The Koran does not give much specific advice on economic matters, so debates on what a truly Islamic economy should be are common. Conservative leaders are against any reform, but Khatami, who is considered a pragmatist, steers a more moderate course.

Measures to revive the Iranian economy in the 1990s included the privatization of state enterprises, the reopening of the Tehran Stock Exchange, and the liberalization of foreign exchange regulations. More liberal investment policies have also been introduced.

In 2002 Iran made a transition to a unified floating foreign exchange rate. This, coupled with reduced corporate tax rates, is helping to make Iran more attractive to foreign investors.

Although Iran still depends heavily on its oil and gas exports, the percentage of non-oil exports has grown dramatically since the 1990s. Apart from oil and gas, Iran's chief export items are carpets, fruit, and

TRADING IN THE BAZAAR

Much of modern Iranian trade is conducted in the manner of Western industrialized nations. Business is done in offices and shops, by telephone and fax machines. Goods are distributed on trucks, trains, ships, and planes. But one feature that gives Iranian trade a local color is the bazaar.

Though there are air-conditioned shopping centers in the cities, bazaars are still important places for selling and buying goods. Street bazaars are usually under cover of canvas or firmer structures to provide protection from the sun, wind, and weather. The bazaars in the present capital city Tehran and in a former capital city Esfahan are particularly famous and picturesque.

caviar. Iran's major trade partners include Italy, France, Germany, and Japan. Iran and Germany have had a long trade partnership, despite a few rough patches. Since the late 1990s, when Iranian leaders were accused of the assassination of four Kurdish dissidents in Berlin, both nations have been working to rebuild bilateral ties. One step was made in 2000, when Khatami visited German president Johannes Rau to discuss trade and other matters.

While the U.S. embargo that was reaffirmed in 2002 may dampen Iran's future trade prospects, many Asian and European countries are still willing to trade with Iran for a share in its oil and gas reserves.

TOURISM

Many travelers visit Iran for its architecture (including its grand mosques), its history (archeological sites such as Persepolis), and its traditional arts (at handicraft bazaars and museum exhibitions).

Although Iran's conservative leaders worry about the cultural influence of foreign tourists on the citizens of the country, the official stand on tourism remains one of welcome. Iran aims to take advantage of the economic potential of its tourism industry by developing tourist facilities, such as information centers and guides and translators.

Most tourists to Iran come from neighboring countries such as Saudi Arabia and Azerbaijan, while Germans make up the largest number of Western tourists. The number of tourist arrivals from the West has fallen since the September 11 terrorist attacks in the United States.

Sturgeon from the Caspian Sea. Sturgeon eggs are one of Iran's most valuable exports.

ENVIRONMENT

IRAN SITS ON A HIGH PLATEAU, surrounded by mountains, with the Persian Gulf to the south and the Caspian Sea to the north. Archeologists believe that nomads have been living in the region for nearly 100,000 years. Perhaps around 7000 B.C., some nomads settled down with their herds of animals and began farming crops.

In a land where the climate was hot and water scarce, these small populations managed to survive. In the last century, however, high population growth, rapid urban expansion, and the demands of a modernizing economy have posed serious challenges to Iran's natural environment—challenges that persist and that threaten to worsen, unless strong measures are taken, in the 21st century.

AIR POLLUTION

Air pollution is a serious health problem in the capital and other major cities. The main source of pollutants is traffic. Nearly a quarter of the cars in Tehran are over 20 years old. These cars have poor exhaust systems and use low-grade leaded fuel. Sometimes the air gets so bad in Tehran that schools have to close and people have to wear masks or stay indoors. Surrounded by mountains, the city gets trapped in smog. The pollution also affects mountain wildlife.

Since 2000 Iran has been unfolding a 10-year plan to reduce air pollution in the capital. Efforts include phasing out older vehicles and improving public transportation. A new subway network has been constructed to ease road traffic. The authorities have come up with a number of ways to limit traffic, such as encouraging people not to drive on "National Clean Air Day" and allowing only private cars with permits to enter the city center during peak hours.

Opposite: **A decorated garden with a pool in Shiraz for the tomb of the Persian poet Hafiz.**

WATER POLLUTION

Pollution has also struck Iran's waters, which include the Persian Gulf, the Caspian Sea, and many of the country's lakes and rivers. The sources of water pollutants include farms, factories, offshore oil rigs, and coastal housing and tourist resorts.

Most of the world's sturgeon live in the Caspian Sea, where they used to be in abundance. But water pollution and overfishing have reduced sturgeon populations so drastically that these fish are now in danger of extinction.

It is difficult to monitor and regulate the flow of pollutants into the Caspian Sea partly because it is bordered by several countries. Pollutants may enter the sea via, for example, Russia's Volga river or Azerbaijan's Kura river. Finding an effective solution to pollution in the Caspian Sea depends on the cooperation of all the countries involved.

The Persian Gulf is in a similar situation, being one of the major oil-producing regions in the world. Rigs in the gulf drill out 30,000 to 40,000 barrels of oil every day. Some of this oil escapes into the gulf through cracks in the rigs. In addition, waste water released into the gulf by oil companies is high in salt, which raises water temperatures, making it unbearable for fish living in the gulf.

DROUGHT

In August 2000 the Zayandeh Rud river dried up during one of the worst droughts in Iranian history. Major lakes such as the great Bakhtegan shrank, and water in reservoirs around the country fell to very low levels. Iran suffered such severe water shortages that it needed international aid to pull through the devastating drought.

With very little rainfall, drought is a major environmental problem in Iran. Prolonged drought destroys the country's wetlands, the natural habitats of aquatic plants and animals and of birds living in these areas. Wildlife die from starvation and disease, and rural residents lose their means of livelihood as their crops and livestock die.

To respond to droughts such as the one in 2000, Iran has built huge dams to control the storage and distribution of water. Dam construction has brought about other environmental problems, such as creating breeding grounds for disease in stagnant water. Dams built on rivers also hinder the movement of fresh water into the gulf, thus worsening the plight of the gulf's fish population.

A hotel near the Si-o-Se Pol (33 Arches Bridge), which spans the Zayandeh Rud river.

THREAT TO BIODIVERSITY

The term biodiversity, or biological diversity, refers to the variety of plants and animals that live in a specific area. A major environmental challenge in many countries is protecting this natural diversity from the harmful activities of modern society. The danger is especially great for endemic plant and animal species, which are unique to a country or region and cannot be found in any other part of the world.

Deforestation takes place where trees are cleared to make space for housing and to provide fuel or raw materials for construction and paper manufacture. Desertification, or the expansion of desert land, occurs where fields are overgrazed or where farmers use poor cultivation techniques. Deforestation and desertification have led to the extinction of several plants and animals in Iran.

As Iran's human population grows, more and more land is taken over for housing and farming—over 230 square miles (596 square km) of forests are cleared each year. Wild animals that lose their home this way have to compete for food with domesticated animals, but they are often killed by farmers.

To protect Iran's natural environment, the government has embarked on reforestation programs and sand dune stabilization efforts to control desertification. There are also laws aimed at protecting plants and animals and fighting pollution, such as the Environmental Protection and Enhancement Act.

Opposite: **Thorny Astragalus grow wild in the Zagros Mountains.**

HOPE FOR IRAN'S VANISHING ANIMALS?

Among Iran's threatened animal species is the Baluchestan black bear, a subspecies of the Asiatic black bear. Asiatic black bears, close cousins of the American black bear, have larger ears and a V-shaped white patch on the chest. The Baluchestan black bear was once thought to be extinct, but was later rediscovered and is now considered critically endangered. It lives in forested areas near waterholes in the arid southern regions of Iran: Kerman, Hormozgan, and Baluchestan. Deforestation has greatly reduced the bears' natural habitat, and farmers kill them to protect their livestock and crops.

The Caspian tiger once lived in parts of the Middle East and Russia. Forest clearing near the Caspian Sea to make way for farming forced the tiger out of its natural habitat. Unable to adapt as well to other areas, the Caspian tiger gradually disappeared and is now believed to be extinct. The Iranian lion had the same fate. Originally living in the southern Zagros Mountains, the lion was hunted for sport by royalty, one of the main causes of the lion's extinction. Meanwhile, Iran's cheetah and leopard populations are dwindling, while jackals and hyenas are fighting for survival against human encroachment into their natural habitats.

Persian fallow deer once roamed a large part of the Middle East and northeastern Africa. They have been thought to be extinct a few times in the past, only to be rediscovered in a secluded location. In the 1950s, a small population was found in a forested area in western Iran, near the border with Iraq. Laws were put in place to conserve the remaining Persian fallow deer, but since the war with Iraq in the 1980s, it is not known for certain how many are left. It is classified as endangered and remains one of the world's rarest deer species.

There is hope for some of Iran's threatened species if prompt and proper action is taken to protect them. The yellow deer, for example, is no longer on the threatened species list (it has not gone into the extinct species list). After efforts by the government and by conservationists, the yellow deer population is growing.

A green scene in the southern Zagros region, where sheep and goat herds graze. One major conservation effort here involves preventing or remedying the consequences of overgrazing —erosion and desertification.

PROTECTING THE ENVIRONMENT

Under Iran's constitution, protecting the environment is considered a public duty, and surveys have shown that Iranians care strongly about the environment. However, political instability due to a revolution and a war have hindered conservation efforts until recently. Conservation is now a major priority in government policy. National parks and wildlife refuges have been established, and fish culture programs are helping to replenish dwindling sturgeon populations in the Caspian Sea.

Due to an increasing population and rapid modernization, energy consumption in Iran has tripled since 1980. This has been a major contributor to the country's pollution problem. The destructive effects of rising energy consumption on the natural environment are wide-ranging and long-lasting. Apart from producing more pollutants through the burning of fossil fuels, it places a heavy strain on Iran's enormous yet limited fuel resources. (The government is considering alternative forms of energy, such as solar, wind, and tidal power. Nuclear energy is also being explored, despite international opposition.) Another way oil and gas exploration has damaged the environment is through the use of massive machines to dig into the earth, sometimes under mountains.

Environmental groups such as the Green Party of Iran and the Green Front of Iran have to work within tremendous political and economic constraints, while Iran is still adjusting politically and socially and has limited financial resources. The biggest challenge for the country is to balance economic development with environmental protection.

An oil refinery at the port of Bandar-e Abbas on the Persian Gulf coast.

IRANIANS

IRAN HAS A POPULATION of more than 66.6 million people. Most Iranians live in the northern part of the country, where the capital is located. Central Iran, with its hills and deserts, is sparsely populated. Climate plays a role in population density and the way social life is structured in Iran. As in much of the Middle East, people from the harsh desert and semi-desert environments tend to live and group together differently than those from the lush, fertile coastal areas and valleys.

Iranians are known for their hospitality, which stems partly from the fragility of life in a harsh land, where people have to depend on one another for many of their basic needs.

Left: **An Iranian family in Esfahan.**

Opposite: **Two girls in traditional dress in Yazd.**

TRIBES AND CLANS

Among nomads, the basic unit of a community is the tribe, usually ruled by a chieftain. There are also tribes that have settled in villages. However, nomads generally consider themselves superior to villagers, so they will always acknowledge their nomadic background and ancestry.

A nomadic campsite is made up of the tents of the families of the tribe. The tent protects the family from the desert winds and is surrounded by a fence to keep out wild animals. The tents and fences are collapsible and can be easily mounted on horses or camels whenever the tribe moves to greener pastures or to look for water at oases.

A Kurdish family in their tent. The Kurds are a nomadic tribe in Iran. Their traditional clothing reminds us of that of the gypsies of Europe.

Within a nomadic tribe, there are elaborate customs dictating each person's behavior, lines of authority among members of the tribe, and marriage patterns between families. These customs are necessary to maintain strong family bonds and to preserve the tribal structure.

In the villages, the most important social groups are the clan and the family. A few interrelated families ma ke up a clan. Each family may live in a mud-brick home in the village compound.

Many villages in Iran consist of just one clan, while larger villages may have several clans. Within the clan, one's family comes first. Loyalty to the family is important in the villager's daily life and even for his or her survival.

Families in a clan usually work together and mingle in their daily social activities. They share whatever good fortune or bad luck comes their way. Thus village communities tend to be tight-knit and united, with a strong sense of belonging to the clan.

Mud-brick rooms around a vast courtyard typical of many villages in Iran. Each room may house a whole family.

A Qashqa'i chieftain's wife parades the wealth of her community.

URBANIZATION AND TRADITION

In Iran's cities, the tribe and clan have lost almost all of the significance they have in nomadic and village communities. In the cities, the role of tribe and clan is taken over by the extended family—a network of blood relations that includes grandparents, aunts, uncles, and cousins. Although urban Iranian families may not always live together under one roof, they do take one another's concerns very seriously.

The average Iranian family is getting smaller as healthcare improves and living standards rise. While the average number of children per family in Iran—about six—is still very high when compared to families in the Western world, the figure is still lower than that in most other Middle Eastern countries.

Despite growing Western influences, especially in the cities, Iranians have maintained a strong sense of family. They visit one another, spend quality time together, and talk over family dinners. Religious values and customs persist, especially in rural areas. In a traditional Muslim family, divisions exist by gender. For instance, there are areas of the house for family and areas where unrelated male guests are entertained by male family members.

The practice of polygamy—Islamic law allows a man to take four wives—is gradually declining. While a man can divorce his wife anytime, a woman needs her husband's written permission to file for divorce. However, women's divorce rights in Iran are being reviewed.

Young Iranian women in Tehran enjoy some ice cream together.

A shy Persian girl.

ETHNIC GROUPS

Iran is a multiethnic society of mainly Persians, Azeri, Kurds, Arabs, Baluchis, Lur, and Turks. Nomadic minorities and foreigners constitute a very small percentage of the population. The largest ethnic groups are the Persians, who make up half of the population, and the Azeri, who account for 24 percent of Iranians.

PERSIANS The Persians have their origins in an ancient culture. They are an Indo-European people, whose ancestors are believed to have come from Central Asia around 2000 B.C. From around 550 B.C. Persia became a powerful empire and ruled vast territories as far as India.

Persians today are proud of their history, immortalized in monuments from the various periods of Persian rule that can still be seen throughout the country, especially in Persepolis and Esfahan. When Iran's original name, Persia, was replaced in 1935, it signified the nation's transition into a new era of modernity, but also acknowledged its Persian roots, for "Iran" was derived from the ancient Persian language.

One attribute that identifies the Persians with other peoples of the Middle East is their shared religion, Islam. Yet the Persians have their own ethnic profile and culture, distinct from that of Arab and other Middle Eastern cultures.

AZERI AND KURDS Together the Azeri and the Kurds account for 31 percent of the Iranian population. These groups predominate in northwestern Iran. They have made several bids for autonomy and supported the revolution, hoping that the removal of the shah would improve their position in Iranian society—it did not. Khomeini continued the shah's trend to invest ultimate authority in the government, with one difference: he abolished democratic representation of various groups and peoples.

There are also Kurds in Iraq and Turkey. Yet no matter where they live and whether as nomads or urbanites, they have managed to look after their own communities and to maintain their own language and religion.

A group of Iranian boys.

ARABS Iran has a significant Arab population, concentrated in the southern province of Khuzestan. In fact, there are so many Arabs living here that some neighboring Arabic-speaking nations do not regard this region as being part of Iran. The Iraqis, for instance, still refer to the area as Arabestan, its name before Iran occupied it in the 1920s, and the province was a major point of contention in the Iran-Iraq war. Khuzestan is important to Iran because it is rich in oil deposits.

Ethnic conflict has flared up occasionally, such as during the 1979 revolution. The Arabs demanded local autonomy, a greater share of the oil revenue, and an end to discrimination. Arabs in Iran feel that they are not getting a fair share of income or employment or a voice in politics.

Opposite: **A Baluchi man weaves cord from leaves.**

Below: **Kurds celebrate a wedding in Iran.**

NOMADS

Some estimates put the size of Iran's nomadic and semi-nomadic population at 3 to 4 percent of the total population, while others put it as high as 13 percent.

This variation is partly due to different definitions of nomads: some move freely their entire lives; others follow a set path and area; yet others have established homesteads in a few locations.

Most nomads are organized in tribes, such as the Bakhtiari, Baluchi, Lur, and Khamseh. Politically, the role of nomads has not been an easy one. Every Iranian ruler has tried to harness nomadic tribes and settle them in fixed locations. This effort has in recent decades achieved only partial success. The nomads remain largely self-sufficient: their herds provide them with food and milk, hair or wool to spin yarn and weave clothes and carpets, and hides to make tent covers.

The proverb "where thy carpet lies is thy house" has true meaning in nomadic life. Many nomads get by without using money. The few goods they want, they barter for in town markets in exchange for their rugs or milk.

Nomads travel along a traditional route through desert and mountain passes that provides water and shelter until they reach a more permanent campsite.

QASHQA'I Over the last two centuries, one nomadic group in particular has acquired some political significance. These are the Qashqa'i, who live in the area around Shiraz and who have their own confederacy. During the early years of the modern state of Iran, the existence of subgroups such as the Qashqa'i, with their own laws, leaders, and independence, was seen as a threat.

In 1979 several leaders of the Qashqa'i, called khans, returned from exile once they knew that the shah had been overthrown. They generally commanded authority among their own people, and some of them became very popular and charismatic leaders in the revolution. Initially they supported Khomeini, who was not quite as generous, having regarded the Qashqa'i as feudal barons and highway robbers.

Once the revolution was won, Khomeini crushed the political power of the Qashqa'i. In 1982 small groups of Qashqa'i in the mountains of southwestern Iran continued to defend themselves against Khomeini's Revolutionary Guard.

In traditional dress that reminds us of the civilization of ancient Persia, a Qashqa'i girl performs a whirling dance during a tribal festivity.

LIFESTYLE

IN TEHRAN, people are generally up and about by 7 A.M., ready for the hustle and bustle of a workday in the city. Shops on the streets open for business, selling newspapers and hot beverages. Factories operate from 7 or 7:30 A.M., while government offices open at 8 A.M. and banks at 8:30 A.M. The average work day for employees in commercial offices is usually eight hours long, while small business owners typically work 10 hours a day. School starts at 8 A.M.

A common work practice in Iran is an extended lunch break, usually two hours long, whether in government offices, factories, or schools and universities. In the summer months, the lunch break may be even longer, but people work later into the evening.

Some workers lunch at restaurants and then take a nap in a park or at home. Most go home to have lunch with their family. This way, family members get to see one another not just in the evening but in the day as well. The self-employed also have an extended lunch break, often four hours long in the middle of the day, as shops tend to stay open until 10 P.M. so that their customers can shop after work.

Friday is the day of prayer, so government offices, banks, and schools close from Thursday afternoon through the whole of Friday. The self-employed also close their shops for at least half the day to take a break from their businesses and go to the mosque.

Above: **A rural Iranian makes traditional bread for the family.**

Opposite: **Urban Iranians enjoy the peace of a park in Esfahan.**

63

RURAL LIFE

Despite the gradual migration of Iranians to the cities, there are still thousands of small villages scattered around the country. These isolated communities have managed to preserve many of their traditional customs and to sustain their old way of life amid technological change in the modernized parts of the country.

In the countryside, life's rhythm is dictated by the seasons and the time of day. Small villages, especially those in inaccessible areas, have no electricity, heating, or piped water. Human activity, like much of nature's activity, follows the sun, starting as it rises and ending as it sets. Oil lamps provide some—but not enough—light in the evening for villagers to spin yarn or weave carpets. Similarly, most of the other daily chores have to be completed during the day: clothes have to be washed and dried, food has to be cooked, water has to be carried from the village well, the fields have to be tended and the animals fed, and so on.

While many villages still depend on manual and animal labor, others have started to experience a little luxury as machines such as tractors are gradually introduced to rural Iran.

Rural Iranians wash their family's clothes at rivers and wells.

EDUCATION

In the 1960s the Iranian government undertook large-scale reforms to improve public education. Many schools, teacher-training institutes, and universities were built during this period. Student enrollment in public schools increased, the quality of education improved, and literacy levels rose. In the 1970s universities in the major cities were expanded.

However, developments in the education system benefited people in the cities more than it did villagers, resulting in an urban-rural literacy disparity. There is also a male-female disparity, with a higher literacy rate for men than for women. Apart from the traditional view that women do not need formal education, women also face legislative barriers to entry into foreign universities.

Elementary school is compulsory for children ages 6 to 12, but some children do not attend, either because the school is too far away or they have to work in the family business or on the family farm. High school is not compulsory and is generally free of charge. Every high-school year finishes with major examinations. Should a student fail a subject (out of as many as 12), he or she has to repeat the entire year.

The school week starts on Saturday morning at 8 A.M. and finishes on Thursday at lunchtime. The school year begins in September and, except for a two-week holiday in March for the New Year, carries on until June the following year without a break. About 95 percent of Iranian children are enrolled in schools, most in government-run schools. In recent years, private schools have sprung up to cater to the wealthy. Getting a place in one of the state universities is not easy; more than a million students attend private universities. Many wealthy Iranians send their children to study in Europe and even as far away as Australia.

Lacking adequate facilities and resources, Iran's education sector is ill-equipped to handle the demand from a large, young population and has far to go in trying to catch up with education in many other countries.

Schoolgirls go home after class. In line with Islamic beliefs, schools in Iran are segregated according to gender.

CITY LIFE

Iran has grown increasingly urban since the middle of the 20th century. By 1988 more than half the total population were living in urban areas, which experienced an annual growth rate twice that in rural areas. By the same year, around 18 million people were living in 40 cities with populations of more than 100,000. By 2000 cities such as Esfahan, Tabriz, and Shiraz had populations of at least 1 million. Population expansion has been fastest in Tehran, the capital, where some 10 million people live, making it Iran's most populous city.

Despite having large populations, Iran's big cities manage to keep open spaces and elegant avenues lined with trees. Rows of small specialized shops border the pavements. There are also multilevel supermarket complexes in the bigger cities. Iranian cities can generally be classified as traditional or modern cities.

TRADITIONAL CITIES The traditional city is easily recognized by three features. First, there is a mosque in the center, usually at the intersection of two major through roads. This mosque is not just a place for prayer; with its large courtyard, it also serves as a meeting place for groups of people. Second, near the mosque are the city government buildings or the palace where a ruler used to live. Third, small streets branch out in all directions from the city center, with at least one serving as the main bazaar area of the city.

The traditional city is thus structured with its center as a hub of faith, power, and trade. Streets tend to be very congested with people on their way to the mosque and to the markets, where livestock, produce, and other goods are sold and bought.

In traditional cities, some Iranians earn a living by making crafts.

In Iran, bazaars are more than places of trade; they have a distinct cultural and historical significance. Iran's bazaars continue to function much as they have for centuries. They have been studied by architects as models of organized structure and design.

Each bazaar is arranged in a logical layout, with rows and alleys that separate stores selling specific items. Products such as carpets, fabrics, jewelry, pottery, or spices are displayed in different sections within the bazaar complex. Bazaar life stimulates the senses with food smells, the sounds of buyers bargaining, the colors of traditional handicrafts, and the nonstop movement of people and animals.

MODERN CITIES In the modern city, much of the raw, intimate atmosphere of the traditional city is gone. One of the main differences, compared to the traditional city, is that the modern city is not people-centered; instead, it is car-centered. In Tehran, boulevards are often eight lanes wide. In the business center, with its administrative buildings, are hotels, cinemas, restaurants, and department stores.

TRAFFIC

Despite having wide streets, Iran's larger cities still suffer from traffic congestion and its consequent dangers. Driving in Tehran can be a nightmare—drivers do not always stop at traffic lights and rarely give signals to let others know what they intend to do. The resulting frenzy, made very audible by the constant tooting of horns, often causes traffic jams that can take hours to unravel.

To deal with road problems in the capital, the Tehran Traffic Control Company was set up in 1991. It uses a traffic management system based on a modern communications network to monitor and control the flow of traffic and reduce the occurence of accidents. Another way to ease the traffic problem is to encourage people to take the bus or train to work instead of driving their own cars.

Driving in the countryside is far easier, though buses and herds of animals may slow the pace. Gravel roads are generally rutted, and the distances between gasoline stations are long—62 miles (100 km) or more

apart. There are also paved highways in the countryside, which makes travel a little faster.

Planned housing in Tehran.

HOUSING

Urban housing by necessity tends to be more compact and carefully planned than rural housing. The type and style of housing and materials used in construction also differ.

THE CITIES Living costs can be extremely high in Iran's large cities. In Tehran, for example, professionals may spend as much as half their salaries on their housing rents, leaving very little for other expenses.

Essentially, Iran's urban housing situation is no different than that in many other countries. City people tend to be neither very rich nor very poor, and they live in relatively modest accommodation. The problem of overcrowding in Iranian cities is made worse by the large size of many families.

THE VILLAGES Thirty percent of the Iranian population still work in agriculture and live in villages. The problem of housing does not arise because many families own property.

Largely because of a limited supply of timber or other building materials, and partly due to the hot climate, houses in the villages are usually made of mud bricks. Ninety percent of all village constructions in Iran are made of mud bricks. Mud bricks are often regarded as building material for the poor, being cheap and readily available. Mud bricks are also useful because mud helps to keep the house cool in summer and warm in winter.

In addition, houses in desert or semi-desert areas usually have wind towers that trap wind and circulate the air to cool the house. The downside is that mud-brick houses cannot withstand earthquakes —they collapse easily.

Partly because of sandstorms, villagers usually build their homes close together. A large clay wall surrounds the village, and inside is a maze of small lanes leading to the various homes. The wall has several purposes: it helps the villagers defend themselves against bandits and shields them from the elements—sandstorms, the cutting cold winter winds, and the strong winds of Central Asia that can blow at 124 miles per hour (200 km per hour) and last more than 100 days. Villages near the Caspian Sea do not have this high wall, as the plentiful vegetation there prevents winds from gaining such speed and destructive force.

There is no running water and no electricity in these villages. There is often only one real street in the village, which has a water channel, or *djuba* (ZHOO-bah), built in the middle. This is the main water supply and the lifeline of the entire village. The position of the *djuba* makes it difficult for an outsider to steal any of the village's water without being seen. Each family in the village enjoys privacy in their small enclosed

A typical Iranian village with its main street lined by mud-brick houses.

courtyards. Inside a house, there is little furniture. Rugs are placed on the clay floor or hung as wall hangings.

Many villages in Iran accommodate just one clan of around 30 to 50 inhabitants. The harsh conditions of the desert—poor soil, too little water—make it difficult to support a larger community. Farming in the Iranian countryside is very hard work, and many villagers live at subsistence levels.

With its mountain villages, coastal villages, and desert villages, the Iranian countryside exhibits an interesting and beautiful array of architectural styles that demonstrate how well people have adapted to their natural environment.

LIFE EXPECTANCY

Life expectancy in Iran improved dramatically during the 1990s. It currently stands at 70 years, only slightly lower than Western life expectancy figures. There is, however, a high infant mortality rate. Some 28 deaths per 1,000 live births, or nearly 3 percent, is quite high when compared to less developed nations at 1 percent or less.

An elderly street vendor.

An extended family in Kordestan.

Iranians do not enjoy pensions, and there is little welfare for the aged. Care for the old is entirely in the hands of the family. As families are large and people spend a lot of time with their families even in the cities, it is natural for Iranians to look after their aging parents. They do not perceive this as a burden, but as a responsibility and a way to show gratitude. The aged are traditionally highly respected. They are seen as holding the keys to wisdom and to family stability, and it is therefore regarded as proper and beneficial for Iranians to live with and care for their aging relatives.

RELIGION

ISLAM is the fastest-growing religion in the world, with approximately 1 billion followers on all five continents.

Nearly all Iranians are Muslims; 89 percent of the total population belong to the Shi'a group, and 10 percent belong to the Sunni group. Zoroastrians, Christians, Jews, and Baha'i worshipers make up 1 percent of the population.

Through its long history in Iran, Islam has molded Iranian culture and influenced people's values, attitudes, and behaviors. More than that, Iran is a religious state. That means that religious rules (in this case, Islamic rules) are synonymous with state rules. It is the teachings of Islam, as interpreted by Khomeini and his followers, that determine state life. Islam influences every aspect of people's lives, such as marriage laws, food practices, work hours, and school uniforms.

Left: **The Royal Mosque of Esfahan, built in the 17th century by Shah Abbas, is a tribute to the glory of Persia and a testament to the faith of its people.**

Opposite: **Beautiful tile work covers the wall and ceiling of this chamber in the Masjid-e Imam (Imam Mosque) in Esfahan.**

LAWS OF ISLAM

Muslims believe that there is only one God. According to the Koran, the basic source of Islamic teaching, God is all-powerful, the creator of everything. Muslims believe that everyone will face a day of judgment, when God will decide if they have led good or bad lives on earth and accordingly send them to heaven or hell.

The Koran emphasizes the social dimension of service to God. It sets forth general ethical and legal principles to guide all aspects of Islamic living. The Koran does not constitute a comprehensive code of laws, but it does include rules on a broad variety of matters, including modesty,

Muslims pray outdoors in Tehran.

marriage, divorce, adultery, fornication, inheritance, intoxicants, diet, gambling, feuding, theft, and murder.

The Koran is not the only source of Islamic laws. The Sunna (SOON-nah) forms the other indispensable guide to the Islamic faith and legal system. It includes all the known sayings of the Prophet Muhammad, his decisions, and his responses to life situations and to philosophical and legal questions.

Six collections of Sunna written in the ninth and 10th centuries are accepted as authoritative by most Muslims. Analogical reasoning and community consensus are the other official sources of Islamic law recognized in classical Islamic jurisprudence. Over the centuries, Islamic laws have evolved and changed, but the main sources of law have remained the same.

THE FIVE PILLARS OF ISLAM

Islam imposes five practices on its followers:
- The declaration of faith—that there is no God but Allah and that Muhammad is the messenger of God
- Prayer: Muslims pray five times a day—at dawn, noon, mid-afternoon, sunset, and nightfall—reciting verses from the Koran. They may congregate at a mosque or pray at home or at their place of work.
- Almsgiving: Muslims make donations to charity every year.
- Fasting: Muslims abstain from food and other worldly pleasures from dawn to dusk during the month of Ramadan.
- The pilgrimage to Mecca: every adult Muslim who is physically and financially able is expected to make this pilgrimage once in their lifetime.

A Sufi cleric in prayer.

SHI'A VERSUS SUNNI

The main difference between the Shi'a and Sunni sects of Islam is that Sunni Muslims recognize the claim of successors, or caliphs, who were not related to the Prophet Muhammad, while Shi'a Muslims do not acknowledge this claim.

The rift between the Sunni and Shi'a groups formed early in Islamic history. One of the chief points of argument was what to do after the death of the Prophet Muhammad in A.D. 632. The Shi'a Muslims of Persia argued that only Muhammad's son-in-law, Ali, had the right to be regarded as the lawful heir and successor and to rule the Muslim community after Muhammad's death.

However, there were some Muslims who opposed this claim, and the strongest opponents became the first Sunni Muslims. A Sunni caliphate was established, and the Sunni Arabs conquered new territory and expanded over time, gaining new converts along the way.

Today, some 90 percent of all Muslims belong to the Sunni branch of Islam. Shi'a Islam, though, is the national religion of Iran. While other points of contention evolved between Sunni and Shi'a Muslims over time, the original dispute is one of the biggest differences.

Another major development in Islam was the controversial religious mysticism called Sufism that began in the ninth century. Sufi Muslims seek to enter into very close union with God through ecstatic worship.

THE *AYATOLLAH*, *MULLAH*, AND *ULEMA*

The Islamic religion claims not to have a hierarchy of authority and priesthood. However, the learned men—the *ayatollah* (AY-yah-toh-lah), *mullah* (MOO-LAH), and *ulema* (uh-LAH-mah)—have become unchallenged political, social, and spiritual leaders.

Applying the teachings of Islam in the fast-changing world of the 21st century brings many new challenges, such as addressing the relevance of religion to modern life and how one can remain true to one's religion in the face of significant social and economic changes.

A *mullah* on the streets of Esfahan.

THE IMPACT OF RELIGIOUS LAWS

After the Islamic Revolution of 1979, the government banned imported meat, luxury goods, and alcohol. In the 1980s music was condemned as a seducer, a distraction from serving God, and cinemas were shut down. Under religious laws, any behavior or deed that is regarded as morally dangerous has stiff penalties imposed upon it. For instance, alcohol consumption, drug abuse, and homosexuality are punishable by death. In spite of this, Iranian film and theater flourished in the late 1990s and some Western musical instruments were allowed into Iran.

Not all Iranians agree with these rules. However, Islam has brought about one unity in Iranian life—all work stops when it is time to pray. Shi'ism in Iran underwent a profound transformation in the 1960s. As it became a political force that eventually helped to overthrow the last shah, it also became more than religious belief, but also a way of life.

WOMEN AND ISLAM

Although Islam teaches that men and women be treated equally, in practice this does not happen. In Iran millions of women participated in the revolution, contributing to its success. But in the aftermath, Khomeini introduced strict laws that greatly curtailed their freedom. For instance, within the family, women had no rights over their children and no protection against domestic violence.

In the 1990s women formed many groups pushing for greater rights in education, work, and marriage. Rising literacy levels since the revolution have helped women to see that there are options. Many Iranian women now work outside the home, such as in teaching and medicine, and nearly half of university students are women. However, laws segregate them so that they can only deal with other women.

Despite the growing participation of women in public life, there are considerable obstacles to further reform. For example, in 2001, when the parliament voted to give Iranian women the same rights as men to study abroad, the conservative Council of Guardians rejected the proposal. The conservatives have also arrested some women's rights activists.

The law requiring women in Iran to wear the *chador* was reintroduced after the revolution. Today, there is more flexibility in the colors of clothing women can wear as long as they cover the head and body.

OTHER RELIGIONS AND SECTS

THE BAHA'I The Baha'i religion originated in Iran in the 19th century. It was started by an Iranian religious visionary, Mirza Ali Muhammad, who called himself Bab, meaning gate. His follower, Mirza Husain Ali (1817–92), was responsible for spreading the movement and gathering more believers. He took the title Baha Ullah (BAH-HAH oo-LAH), meaning Glory of God.

A Baha'i temple, shaped like a lotus blossom.

Baha'i worshipers believe that the Baha Ullah is the latest in a series of divine manifestations that include Jesus, Muhammad, Zoroaster, and the Buddha.

In the Baha'i faith, there are no initiation ceremonies, sacraments, or clergy. Every Baha'i worshiper is required to pray daily, fast for 19 days a year, abstain from drugs and alcohol, and practice monogamy. And a Baha'i couple needs their parents' consent before marriage.

To Muslims, Baha'i believers are traitors to the "true faith." The Baha'i believe that the Messiah has already come. They criticize some of Muhammad's teachings as outmoded, such as the legal inequalities of the sexes and of creeds, polygamy, and

p84: **The altar of the Bethlehem Church in Esfahan.**

the prejudice against music. The Baha Ullah taught that religious truth is not absolute but relative and that each age has to modify and adapt the teachings through new wisdom.

The Baha'i religion was introduced to the Western world in the 1890s. Since then Baha'i temples have been built in the United States, Germany, Australia, Panama, and Uganda. The international Baha'i governing body is known as the Universal House of Justice. It is located in Haifa, Israel, and serves as the supreme administrative, legislative, and judicial body of the Baha'i commonwealth.

The Baha'i faith has not been tolerated in Iran particularly since the revolution. The religion has been prohibited and fought in every way. Despite the persecution, there are still some Baha'i living in Iran today.

THE GHULAT The Ghulat are an extremist Shi'a sect present not only in Iran but also in Iraq, Syria, and Turkey. The Ghulat go by several names: Ahl-i Haqq (ahl-e HACK), or truth worshipers; Ali Ilahis (Ah-li ihl-AH-his), or deifiers of Ali; and Ahl-i Allah (ahl-e AW-LAW), or people of God. As a sect they are very secretive. Their ceremonies are conducted at night in secluded surroundings, a practice dictated at times by the need to avoid persecution. But this has given rise to all sorts of myths about their rituals and beliefs. They meet on Thursday nights and on the first night of the lunar moon, and they make public and private confessions.

One visible difference from mainstream Shi'a is the importance of the moustache. It is said that when the chief disciple, Ali, received instructions from the Prophet Muhammad, he knelt at Muhammad's feet, and his moustache brushed against Muhammad's body. Thus Ali's moustache acquired holiness, and, in allegiance to Ali, no Ghulat today ever clips his moustache.

CHRISTIANS, JEWS, AND ZOROASTRIANS
There are also small numbers of Christians, Jews, and Zoroastrians in Iran. They no longer play a great political or cultural role.

Most Christians in Iran, around 60,000 of them, are members of the Armenian Church. Their largest community is in the Jolfa district at Esfahan. Christians here have their own cathedral, called the Saint Savior Cathedral, where they are allowed to celebrate Sunday Mass. Another Armenian religious center in Iran is the Saint Thaddeus the Apostle Church in Azarbayjan-e Gharbi province. Thousands of Christian pilgrims come here every July. The inhabitants of the region form a community quite firmly set apart from the rest of Iran in language and religion.

Jews in Iran number around 150,000. Some Jews left Iran after the revolution. There are ancient Jewish communities in Iran that have not changed much in their customs since Babylonian times.

Like Christians and Jews, Zoroastrians are recognized as an official religious minority in Iran. Zoroastrians number around 20,000 in Iran. They are followers of an ancient, pre-Islamic religion that continues in isolated areas of Iran today.

ZOROASTRIANISM

Zoroastrianism is an early Aryan faith. It is built on the teachings of the great philosopher Zoroaster. Zoroaster was a prophet and philosopher who lived probably around 600 B.C. He is said to have lived to the age of 77, but he did not die a natural death. He was burned to death because he had criticized the religious orgies and bloody animal sacrifices of the local inhabitants.

Zoroastrianism is based on belief in a supreme deity, Ahura Mazda, and in a cosmic struggle between a spirit of good and a spirit of evil. The ancient Zoroastrians offered sacrifices on mountain peaks, where they built temples. These sacred shrines became their pilgrimage centers. Zoroastrians also worshiped fire as a symbol of God. As a religion, Zoroastrianism has almost died out in Iran.

LANGUAGE

LINGUISTS HAVE IDENTIFIED THREE FORMS of the Persian language: Old Persian, spoken and written by the Achaemenids between the sixth century B.C. and third century A.D.; Middle Persian, used by the Sassanids between the third and 10th centuries A.D.; and New Persian, used since the 10th century and today the language of not only Iranians but also peoples in Afghanistan and Tajikistan.

The name of the language and of the people comes from Pars (Fars in Arabic), an area in the southwest of the Iranian highlands. The ancient Greeks referred to it as Persis. The people called themselves Irani, the Persian name for Aryan.

Persian is an Indo-European language; it belongs to a large family of languages that includes English, German, and French. It is not related to Turkish or Arabic, even though the language is written in Arabic script.

Left: **A biology class in Iran. Adapting the well-established language to include words from modern science is a challenge for linguists today.**

Opposite: **The walls and window of a pizza shop in Esfahan decorated with Arabic script advertising its products.**

NEW PERSIAN

New Persian is the oldest literary language known in the region. Since the ninth century, New Persian has been written using the Arabic alphabet. The written form is very different from the spoken form and is mastered largely by the well-educated. It has remained basically unchanged since the 10th or 11th century and is based on the renowned Iranian epic *Shahnameh*, or *Epic of Kings*, written by one of Persia's greatest poets, Ferdowsi. The *Shahnameh* consists of nearly 60,000 couplets, or pairs of rhyming lines of a verse, which narrate the history of Iran.

Right: **A blue ceramic tile adorned with floral designs and Arabic calligraphy. The word at the center means Allah.**

Opposite: **Calligraphy at the tomb of the Persian poet Sa'di (1184–1291) in Shiraz.**

Arabic calligraphy is written and read from right to left. Many of the letters are flowing and circular and look very attractive. Arabic motifs are abundant in Iran, where the influence of Islam dictates that all works of art be created for the glory of God.

The Persian language was very important in the past. While the first classics of literature were recorded in the 10th and 11th centuries, the Persian language flourished well beyond Persian borders in the 17th century, largely due to the efforts of Shah Abbas. Under him, the empire grew in geographic dimensions and political importance. Since Persia was a world power and a conquering empire, its language became the medium of diplomacy in the entire Middle Eastern and Arab world. Persian also became the language of culture and was spoken in Cairo, Baghdad, and India and at the court of the Turkish sultan in Istanbul.

With the fall of the Persian empire came a decline in the use of its language. But even today, Persian is understood as far as central Asia and India. There are Persian speakers such as the Hazara in parts of Afghanistan, including Kabul and Herat. The language is also used by the Tajik people of Tajikistan. Related literary languages are Kurdish and Baluchi dialects.

A wall mural in Shiraz.

OTHER SPOKEN LANGUAGES

Apart from the national and official language, Persian, spoken by more than half the population, there are other languages and dialects used by smaller groups of Iranians. These include some 16 million Azeri in the northwest, whose language (also called Azeri) belongs to the Turkic language group; around 4.5 million Kurds mostly in the northwest and west, who speak a variety of Kurdish dialects collectively known as Kirmanji; and about 2 million Arabs along the Persian Gulf coast, who speak Arabic, a semitic language. Another semitic language, used by a very small minority in Iran, is Assyrian.

There are also more than a million Lur in southwestern Iran and a similar number of Baluchi in the southeast, who speak languages of the same names. Like Persian, both Lur and Baluchi belong to the Indo-European family of languages.

Like many major languages around the world, Persian is evolving as technological and scientific breakthroughs create new vocabulary.

BODY LANGUAGE

Iranians are a very expressive people, perhaps more so than people are in some Western cultures. Iranians move their hands whether they are excited or exasperated, and emotions of anger, joy, surprise, and pain show readily on their faces. When Iranians want to befriend you, they may hold out their arms toward you.

There are a few Iranian body and hand gestures that differ in meaning from the same gestures in Western countries. For example, what does it mean when a man turns his hand up and waves to himself? In Western cultures, this might simply indicate to the other person to "come here," but in Iran such a gesture, if directed toward a woman, has suggestive motives.

Many of these gestures are influenced by social conventions and religion. Among signals of aggression, the simplest yet most offensive is the thumbs-up. It sends the recipient an insulting message. In direct contrast, the thumbs-up is a positive gesture in the United States, meaning that things are okay, that a job was well done, or that something unusual has been achieved, or it may mean good luck.

While Iranians may be very expressive in their everyday interaction with friends and family members, they are much more formal in larger social spheres than people are in the United States. One barrier lies in gender differences—a major rule in Iran is that men and women should not touch each other. Status differences are also more apparent in Iranian society.

Scribes at their makeshift offices along a street offer paid services to read or write letters.

ARTS

THROUGH THE USE OF SYMBOLS rather than iconic representations, Iran has developed its own unique style of art and architecture. Persian literature, especially poetry, is rich and varied. Persian poets have produced classics that are influential even today and that have attracted the attention of non-Iranians as well. Carpet weaving has almost reached perfection, making the name Persia synonymous with exquisite carpets.

LANDSCAPE GARDENING

The art of landscape gardening probably had its origins in Persia. Cyrus the Great built the world's oldest known garden. It was a carefully planned garden with a pavilion and pools and canals producing the sound of flowing water and providing a soothing background for majestic trees.

Two of the most important trees used by early Persian gardeners were the plane and cypress. The most popular flowering plants were the rose, in all its glorious colors, and the jasmine, which gave a sweet fragrance. Fruit trees and vines, such as figs, dates, grapes, peaches, pears, and pomegranates, were also planted to beautify gardens.

Iran's landscaped gardens mimic the Koranic vision of paradise as a perfect garden with many shady trees, abundant fruit, scented flowers, and rippling water. Shiraz is one of Iran's most beautiful cities, with tree-lined boulevards and landscaped gardens.

LITERATURE

Persian literature peaked between the 10th and 16th centuries, when artists created significant works of philosophy, mathematics, astronomy, medicine, and poetry even though it was a period of wars and internal disorder.

Much of early Persian literature was filled with the visions of a garden paradise with pavilions, nightingales, flowers, and fruit. Poetry is a major aspect of Persian literature. Persia's great poets included Ferdowsi, Hafiz, and Omar Khayyam. Ferdowsi wrote the *Shahnameh* about the lives of legendary kings and heroes as well as actual historical figures. Many copies of this epic poem were illustrated with miniatures by well-known artists. The *Shahnameh* is still a beloved work and has been translated into English.

Hafiz was perhaps the most popular poet. He wrote nearly 700 poems, most of which deal with religious themes. His tomb in Shiraz is a place of pilgrimage for many Iranians seeking inspiration and guidance. They open one of his books and take the first line that catches their eye as a message for them.

Omar Khayyam's poetry is widely read in the Western world, since his collection of poems *Rubaiyat* was translated into English by Edward Fitzgerald in 1858.

Although Khayyam is admired as a poet, he did far more substantial work in mathematics and astronomy. His scientific writing had great influence, and he was selected to be part of the team that did the calculations for the reformed calendar in early 11th-century Persia.

RUBAIYAT

These are excerpts from the *Rubaiyat* of Omar Khayyam, translated from Persian by Edward Fitzgerald.

Ah, make the most of what we yet may spend,
Before we too into the Dust Descend;
Dust into Dust, and under Dust, to lie,
Sans Wine, Sans Song, Sans Singer and—Sans End!

Alike for those who for TODAY prepare,
And those that after some TOMORROW stare,
A Muezzin from the Tower of Darkness cries,
"Fools! Your Reward is neither Here nor There."

Ah, fill the cup: what boots it to repeat
How Time is slipping underneath our Feet;
Unborn TOMORROW and dead YESTERDAY,
Why fret about them if TODAY be sweet!

The Moving Finger writes; and, having writ,
Moves on; nor all the Piety nor Wit
Shall lure it back to cancel half a Line,
Nor all thy Tears wash out a Word of it.

Opposite: **The tomb of the famous Persian poet Hafiz in Shiraz. His name means "one who remembers," and it is said that he knew the entire Koran by heart.**

p96: **A gateway in Persepolis portrays one of its kings, Darius the Great, beside the mythical griffin, or winged lion.**

p97: **A dome in Esfahan with traditional blue tiles. Domes, minarets, and arched windows and doorways reflect the historical and religious significance of architecture in Iran.**

EARLY ARCHITECTURE

The Greek historian Herodotus wrote in detail about early Persian architecture. He gave the world fascinating descriptions of early Persian cities and buildings. Most of these structures were made of brick. There were descriptions of fire temples with fire altars, reflecting the religious beliefs of the early Persians. There were also palaces with fortresses.

The ruins at Persepolis are an outstanding example of Persian architecture. Darius the Great started the building of the capital city in 520 B.C. Succeeding rulers continued his work for nearly a century. The city contained palaces, audience halls, gateways, and other buildings. The expertise of artisans from all over the empire was used in building this magnificent capital. Stone was initially favored as a building material; oven-baked or sun-dried bricks were used later.

Abstract decoration was a major feature of Persian architectural style, especially after the Islamic period. Bricks were laid in a decorative manner, sometimes in high relief, sometimes inset. The effect was an amazingly intricate geometric pattern. Glazed colored tile work was also used to enhance the decorative brickwork.

MOSQUES

The Arab invasion of Iran brought an Islamic influence on Persian architecture, especially between A.D. 641 and 1000. The Islamic house of worship, the mosque, was essentially a large open structure with arcades and a sheltered sanctuary within which a prayer niche directed worshipers to face Mecca, Islam's holiest city, when they prayed. The mosque also had a minaret from which the faithful were called to prayer.

The dome was the most important feature of the mosque. It was built over the principal chamber of the mosque. Because of their awe-inspiring shape, domes took on a symbolic religious significance, and as the years went by the domes became larger in diameter and rose higher and higher. Many of the domes were covered in special blue tiles that sparkled in the sun for all to see. Persian architects also designed methods of erecting domes and vaults without using any supporting columns.

Although Iran's mosques are splendid examples of Islamic Persian architecture, many of the nation's beautiful baths, bridges, palaces, and shrines were also built by Persian architects in the Islamic period.

PAINTING

There are three main features of traditional Persian painting: they are highly stylized, often using abstractions; they are colorful; and they are idealistic. Persian painters are known for their imaginative rendering of flowers, plants, and animals on almost any surface of any size.

Early Persian painting was mostly confined to books. Illustrated books became works of art during the Safavid period, with myths and legends as the favorite subjects for miniature painters. (Many Persian carpet weavers often used figures from miniature paintings, which they enlarged in their carpet designs.)

Early Persian painters rarely signed their names to their work. Hence, unlike the early European painters, very little is known about the pioneers of early Persian painting.

Traditional painters tended to portray an enchanted world of perfection. However, since 1979 the trend in Iranian painting has been to move away from the ideal to more realistic representations. While early paintings depicted kings and their activities, modern paintings show ordinary people in everyday situations. Present-day Iranian painters use their imagination in a wider sense to express different emotions, from joy to sorrow.

POTTERY

The potter's art has existed since 6000 B.C. in Iran. Several distinctive examples of ancient pottery have been found in the province of Khorasan. These are mainly flat bowls with colorless glaze over brightly colored designs.

Other ancient Iranian vessels that have been unearthed include jugs and jars in the shape of various animals such as deer and goats. Archeologists have also uncovered numerous artifacts that are mainly stone carvings of animals and human heads. There are also small animal figures in bronze and other precious metals.

Potters in Iran produced exquisite works during the Islamic period as well. They made earthen utensils, which they painted in many colors and decorated with the images of animals and plants using three techniques: engraving, molding, and embossing.

CALLIGRAPHY

Calligraphy is a special art of writing that is held in great esteem in the Islamic world. God's messages were in Arabic, so Muslims consider the Arabic script sacred and the task of copying out the whole or parts of the Koran in beautiful writing a meritorious act. Many calligraphers enjoy great prestige because of the association of this art form with the Koran.

Above: **Exquisite tilework in a mosque.**

Opposite: **A portrait of a Sufi dervish in Esfahan.**

THE MOST EXPENSIVE CARPET IN HISTORY

The legend behind the carpet of Khosrow II describes the lengths its makers went to in producing the most expensive carpet in history:

Khosrow II was a Sassanid ruler who loved the arts. He commissioned an exquisite carpet for his palace at Ctesiphon, then the capital of Persia. The design for the carpet was astonishing in its realism. It depicted an enormous garden with flowerbeds, trees, and stones. Pure gold and silver threads represented sparkling streams, and precious gems were inlaid to enhance the illusion of springtime. Thus the king could see the colors of spring whenever he entered the room no matter the season.

Unfortunately, the most expensive carpet in history did not last long. When Arab invaders overthrew the Sassanian dynasty, they are said to have cut the carpet into pieces and taken the jewels as part of their war booty.

CARPETS

Persian carpets are famous all over the world. They are designed not only to be comfortable to sit or sleep on, but also as works of art for display in the home.

The Islamic emphasis on geometry and straight lines is not common in Persian carpet designs. Instead, curling flowers and tendrils are more common. Although most Islamic countries banned any artistic representation of living creatures, Iran rejected this ban and Iranian artists used human and animal figures quite frequently in their carpet designs. Traditional Persian carpets of the 16th and 17th centuries were adorned with the images of tweeting birds and sweet-smelling flowers, portraying a beautiful garden to remind them of paradise. (While we are on the subject, the word paradise probably comes from a Persian word associated with the idea of a beautiful garden.)

The color or dye used in carpet making is all-important. Traditionally dyes were made from plants or insects. Here is a list of colors and their symbolic meanings in Persian culture: white for death, mourning, and grief; black for destruction; orange for devotion and piety; red for happiness and wealth; and brown for fertility.

Original handmade Persian carpets fetch very high prices in foreign markets. Each of these carpets has a unique character that cannot be reproduced exactly, not even by the same artist. Cheaper carpets that are mass-produced in factories may imitate original patterns but can never match handmade carpets in their quality and design.

This traditional art of handweaving carpets is a treasure to be passed on from generation to generation. However, many younger Iranians are reluctant to take up this art, preferring the excitement of city life instead. Yet carpet weaving remains the most widespread handicraft in Iran.

A carpet maker at work in Esfahan.

A group of musicians play at a village festival.

IRANIAN MUSIC

Traditionally, musicians in Iran never enjoyed a high social position, although they would play at special events such as weddings and circumcision ceremonies. Stringed instruments often accompanied the singers. Vocal music with improvisation is a very important aspect of traditional Iranian music. The songs are often mournful. At weddings, guests are often entertained by vulgar songs.

Folk music is played in the villages when people celebrate a festival or special family event. Male dancers entertain, sometimes dressed as females. Traditional musicians and groups such as Boushehr's Leymer Folk Music Group perform at annual festivals such as the Fajr Music

Dancers dressed in all their finery perform for a wedding.

Festival, usually held in February, and the Iranian Epic Music Festival, usually held in April.

A special type of music is performed in the traditional wrestling establishment called Zur Khaneh (ZOOR KAH-nah), or House of Power. Drums provide vigorous background music to which verses of poems such as Ferdowsi's *Shahnameh* are sung, as the gymnasts perform feats of strength with heavy paddles.

The ability to recite the Koran is greatly admired. Iranian children are taught at an early age to recite verses from the Koran, and when they grow older, they are encouraged to take part in Koran-reading performances or competitions. These are often held in the fasting month of Ramadan.

Iranians still play many traditional musical instruments. Some of the more popular ones are the sitar, a lute; the *santur* (san-TOOR), a 72-stringed instrument; the *kamenchay* (kah-men-CHAY), a spike-fiddle; the *zarb* (ZAHRB), a goblet-shaped drum; and the *nay* (NAY), a flute. The sitar, popular in northern India, has its origins in Iran.

LEISURE

THE CONCEPT OF LEISURE in Iran differs somewhat from that in other countries. History, religion, and geographical location have helped to create a diverse and varied way of life that is uniquely Iranian.

ENTERTAINING AT HOME

Iranians gladly open their homes to strangers and offer their guests as much as they can afford. The home is the center of all pleasurable activities and the place to go for the best Iranian cooking (not the restaurants). A meal at home with family and friends is often a leisure activity in itself. Iranians usually linger over their meals, discussing their daily affairs.

Drinking is a common social activity, although alcohol has been banned in Iran since the Islamic Revolution of 1979. (Islam prohibits the consumption of liquor.) In place of liquor, and for cultural reasons, tea has become a popular social drink, and the samovar is always on the boil in Iranian homes. Tea-drinking carries deeper social meaning in Iran than in many other countries.

The mass media offer Iranians another avenue for leisure. Listening to the radio and watching television are favorite pastimes, even more popular than reading a book.

Iranians also while the time away by the sea, enjoying the breeze as they recall the good old days.

Above: **Family gatherings are a major leisure activity for many Iranians.**

Opposite: **People stroll past a sculpture in the garden of the Chehel Sutun (40 Columns) Palace in Esfahan.**

TRADITIONAL SPORTS

Horse racing, a sport that goes back centuries, is still a major leisure pursuit in the Iranian countryside today. Although falconry and hunting are not as common as they once were, there are Iranians who continue to train eagles or hawks for the sport of falconry.

Polo and Iranian-style wrestling are other ancient sports that continue to attract many enthusiasts in present-day Iran. Soccer and wrestling are popular spectator sports, while polo tends to have a larger following among wealthier Iranians.

MODERN SPORTS

Iranians had almost no access to modern competitive sports until World War I. When Christian missionaries visited the Middle East, they brought with them Western-style sports. Iranians then began to take an interest in athletics, tennis, basketball, and swimming. Soldiers also encouraged these sports during the two world wars. Soccer became extremely popular, and today children have taken to the sport, kicking a ball in a group along the tree-lined streets of Iran.

Tennis and squash are also popular with Iranians. Squash is a more recent entrant; it is favored by urban Iranians who want to work up a sweat after a long day in the air-conditioned office. Many squash courts have been built to cater to this growing demand.

Gymnastics is actively encouraged in schools, while in the coastal regions more affluent Iranians have taken up sailing.

As in many areas of life, women have limited access to the world of sport in Iran. Only in recent years have women been allowed to attend soccer matches in the major cities. Also, women can carry out their sporting activities only in stadiums or other sporting venues that are specially designated for women. Women also have to follow strict rules about clothing, even in sports.

In spite of these restrictions, some Iranian women have become accomplished athletes. Although they are still not allowed to participate in competitions, they do represent their nation in an all-women Islamic games meet held every year.

Opposite: **Iranian skiers at a ski resort north of Tehran.**

THE SPORT OF SHAHS

Iran and China both developed the sport of falconry more than 3,000 years ago. The art of training falcons, hawks, or eagles requires a lot of patience and skill, as these birds of prey—having natural killer instincts—first have to be tamed to obey the falconer.

Straps are tied around the bird's feet to restrain it, and a hood covers its eyes to keep it calm. Bells are hung round its neck or leg to track its movement. When the falconer sights a potential prey, he removes the hood and releases the bird, which immediately flies in pursuit.

In ancient Persia, falconry was the sport of the shahs and nobility. The wide expanse of the desert was ideal for this sport. Falconry is no longer popular today; shooting has taken its place instead.

POLO

The game of polo, or "horse-ball," began over 2,000 years ago. Two teams of four men on horseback would hit a ball using long sticks. The players had to be skillful riders as they usually played at full gallop. The rule that the ball had to be struck at full gallop was introduced in Iran.

The shahs of Iran loved to watch polo matches seated in the comfort of a pavilion. In fact, it has been said that the city of Esfahan was planned around the royal polo ground. Even today ancient goal posts made from stone stand eight yards apart on the site of the polo square.

Horse-ball eventually found its way to northern India, where British army officers stationed during British rule in India named it polo. The game now known as polo is enjoyed by many all over the world, although it has lost some of its former popularity in Iran.

LEISURE IN THE COUNTRYSIDE

Iranians in the villages make their own entertainment. Their leisure activities are often an extension of their work, so taking joy in their daily activities becomes as much a leisure activity as working for a living.

Most children in Iran's villages help their parents with chores around the house or on the farm during much of the day and take a break in

Above: **Iranian village children at playtime.**

p111: **The cinema also entertains urban Iranians. Western films, popular at one time, are now mostly banned. Most films that Iranians get to watch are from India and Turkey. Censorship is strict.**

the evening, playing simple traditional games that they have learned from their parents and grandparents or simply kicking a ball around. Growing up in a clan community, village children enjoy a lot of contact with same-age cousins and friends.

Traveling troupes are another source of entertainment in the Iranian countryside. A traveling group of actors occasionally goes around the villages reading poetry or performing plays about Iran's past. They tell stories of battles won and lost, of heroes in history.

Snake charmers were once common in the countryside, where people could earn a living by hypnotizing snakes with pipe tunes. Watching a snake charmer is now a rare form of entertainment, perhaps because of the draw of modern media such as radio and television.

Most Iranian villages have a mosque, where many people gather for prayers on Fridays. The mosque is a focal point in the community, and worshipers usually socialize after the prayers.

Sometimes people go to bathhouses to bathe and relax. Bathhouses are built underground at the source of a hot water spring.

Iranians also hold horse races to celebrate festivals and other special occasions.

THE HOUSE OF POWER

The House of Power, or Zur Khaneh as it is known in Iran, is believed to have originated during the Arab invasion of Persia. The House of Power started out as a secret society of young men who swore to drive out the foreign invaders.

Zur Khaneh traditions continue in present-day Iran. Members go through vigorous physical training, doing strenuous exercises to the accompaniment of drumbeats and the chanting of verses from an ancient text. The strong men wield heavy clubs, juggling them around with great speed and dexterity.

A House of Power has one large room containing a wrestling pit. There is a platform for the drummer and a space for spectators. The men wear colorful knee-length trousers. Each session ends with a wrestling match in both traditional and modern European styles.

LEISURE IN THE CITIES

The intense heat in summer compels many Iranians to focus their outdoor leisure in the relative cool of the evening and morning.

Like cafégoers in other parts of the world, people in Iran's modern cities enjoy watching the world go by from their seat in a teahouse called a *kafekhanna* (KAH-FEEK-hah-nah), which actually means coffeehouse.

It is common to see people drinking in a teahouse under a bridge in Esfahan. Teahouses are also the place to smoke a hubble-bubble pipe, or *hookah* (HOO-kah). The smoker inhales smoke through a tube attached to a jar that is partly filled with water. The water cools the smoke before it reaches the smoker's lips.

In the traditional cities, women seldom take part in leisure activities outside the home, as household chores take up much of their time. However, they do get a welcome break from the routine of everyday life with visits to the bazaar or to the mosque, where they get many opportunities for social interaction. Women also enjoy entertaining friends and relatives at home or making handicrafts such as rugs.

Pastimes during winter include listening to music and, especially for wealthier people living in the bigger cities, skiing.

The entrance to a bazaar. Besides bazaars, Iranians can also shop at malls in the larger cities.

OTHER PASTIMES

Many Iranians love a picnic in the park. A rug and some finger food and soft drinks make for a simple outing close to nature. The outdoors can be enjoyed most of the year in the dry climate, if one can bear the heat.

Chess is a well-loved game in Iran. It began in India in about 400 B.C., and when the Iranians took it up soon after, they called the king piece *shah*. It is from this word that the word chess was derived. Similarly checkmate comes from the word *shahmat* (SHAH-mad), meaning the king is helpless.

Religious leaders have banned chess several times because of the associated practice of gambling, forbidden under Islamic law. Despite these occasional decrees, the game always seems to make a comeback.

IRAN'S TOOLS OF LEISURE

Iranians have invented interesting instruments to help them relax. Two of these tools are the samovar and the water pipe. Both have also become "canvases" for the artist, and today there are decorative versions of these practical devices.

THE SAMOVAR The samovar is a metal, usually copper, urn. It is always on the boil in homes, teahouses, government offices, and bazaars. Many Iranians will lug a samovar with them even to a picnic and even on a hot day.

The custom of drinking tea in Iran is a relatively recent event. It was probably introduced from Russia in the 19th century. Before this, most Iranians were coffee drinkers, as were other Muslims in the Middle East. Tea has since replaced coffee as the national drink in Iran. Relaxing over a glass of tea is a favorite pastime. Tea not only quenches one's thirst but also has a relaxing effect.

Tea is seldom served in cups in Iran. Instead, it is served, with plenty of sugar, in small glasses. There is a special way to enjoy tea too: you place lumps of sugar on your tongue and then sip the tea from the glass, drawing in the smell and taste of the strong tea.

THE WATER PIPE The water pipe, or hubble-bubble pipe, consists of a long hose attached to a glass jar that is partly filled with water. The jar is sometimes beautifully decorated, and the water may be flavored with fruit juice. A small dish for tobacco is fitted to the top of the jar.

This is how one smokes the water pipe: first, damp tobacco leaves are placed in the dish, which is then covered with foil; next, a piece of hot coal is placed on top of the foil; when the smoker is ready, he or she inhales from the tip of the hose; smoke from the tobacco leaves is pulled through holes in the dish and into the jar; as the smoke passes through the sweet water in the jar, it gets cooled; the smoke then makes its way through the tube into the smoker's mouth.

Pipe smoking is a very social activity—Iranians go to teahouses in groups and take their time, carrying on long conversations. Both men and women smoke the water pipe. It is a cultural tradition not only in Iran but in other Middle Eastern countries as well.

FESTIVALS

RELIGIOUS FESTIVALS AND HOLIDAYS—and there are many in Iran—are a major part of traditional family life. Most holy days commemorate some aspect of the life and teaching of the Prophet Muhammad. Most Iranians follow a version of Islam called Shi'a, so they commemorate some aspects of the life and teaching of the founders and leaders of this branch of Islam.

Iranians commemorate some religious events with mourning, remembering the suffering of the early leaders of Shi'a Islam, such as Ali ibn Abi Talib, the Prophet's son-in-law and the only rightful successor recognized by Shi'a Muslims. Ali ibn Abi Talib's sons, Hussein and Hassan, also met untimely deaths and never took up leadership after their father's death.

But not all Iranian festivals are Islamic. The New Year festival of Now Ruz (no-ROOS) dates back to pre-Islamic days. Among the ancient traditions that Iranians

practice during the season of Now Ruz is jumping over fires.

Then there are holidays that celebrate important political events in Iran's history since the fall of the shah. These occasions are usually celebrated with much pomp and ceremony, especially in Tehran. Street parties are also part of the celebrations during nonreligious festivals.

Above: **All dressed up for a village festival in Mazandaran in northern Iran.**

Opposite: **Iranians celebrate the 13th day of Now Ruz at a garden concert.**

FESTIVALS OF THE PROPHET

Muslims usually celebrate the Prophet's birthday at a mosque. Special prayers are held, and sometimes a religious leader takes the opportunity to remind the worshipers of their Islamic beliefs and duties. Muslims usually spend the day quietly. At home parents may tell their children stories about Muhammad's life, his parents, and his birth.

Muslims do not commemorate the death of the Prophet in a big way. Instead they celebrate his ascension into heaven. This is called *Leilat al Meiraj* (LAY-lah ahl MEH-RAJ). It is a solemn festival, and sometimes people may visit graves.

EID AL-ADHA

Every year Muslims all over the world perform a sacrificial ritual in remembrance of a holy man's faith in God and his submission to God's will. This is the celebration of Eid al-Adha (eed ahl-AHD-ha), or the feast of the sacrifice.

The festival of Eid al-Adha commemorates Abraham's willingness to sacrifice his son in obedience to God. Abraham is a well-known patriarch among Christians, Muslims, and Jews, who have in common the Old Testament.

The Muslim version of the event tells how Abraham was about to offer his son Ishmael as a sacrifice at Mina, near Mecca, when a voice called out to him to stop. An angel then appeared with a lamb and offered it in place of Abraham's son. Gratefully, Abraham took the animal and sacrificed it.

That is why Muslims commemmorate the event every year with the sacrifice of an animal, usually a lamb or young goat. As Muslims regard all life as sacred, they say prayers and kill the animal in a prescribed way following specific rites. The meat is distributed to the poor.

RAMADAN

Ramadan is the most sacred month in the Islamic lunar calendar. Every day at dawn during this month, Muslims begin a fast. They are allowed to eat and drink again when the last rays of the sun disappear, but they have to start their fast again at the next sunrise. Some Iranians are so strict in observing the fast that they do not even swallow their saliva during the day.

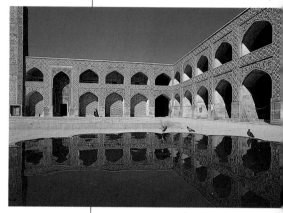

The mosque is where most festivals of religious significance begin.

Shi'a Muslims observe the 21st and 22nd days of the Ramadan month as days of mourning. This is in memory of the martyrdom of Ali ibn Abi Talib, the Prophet's son-in-law. During those two days, devout followers take to the streets beating their breasts and wailing.

The Ramadan month ends with the sighting of the new moon. A religious leader or an elder will usually announce the end of the fasting month. Then begins perhaps the most festive Islamic festival—Eid al-Fitr. Iranian sweets and snacks prepared during the Ramadan month are laid on decorated tables, and everyone is invited to eat as much as they want to relieve the tension of the fast.

Amid the festivities and merrymaking of Eid al-Fitr, Muslims remember the true, spiritual meaning of the event by attending community prayers held either in a mosque or in an open space. Devout Muslims will wash themselves thoroughly and put on clean clothes before going to the prayers. They will also have given alms to the poor or to needy relatives during the month of Ramadan.

When they have fulfilled their religious obligations, Muslims spend the rest of Eid al-Fitr visiting their friends and relatives and feasting on traditional dishes and desserts.

Dancers take a rest during the festivities of Now Ruz.

NOW RUZ

Now Ruz, the Iranian New Year, is celebrated on March 21—the first day of spring. Iranians look forward to this day, hoping for better times. In Iran, as in other countries, anticipation is the name of the game when it comes to celebrating the New Year. However, the traditional way in which Iranians celebrate differs somewhat. The month before Now Ruz is a busy time of preparation. Fifteen days before the festival begins, people plant wheat or lentil seeds in a shallow saucer at home. They herald the first day of spring when they see green shoots emerge from the seeds.

Other activities to prepare for the New Year include spring cleaning. People give their homes a thorough cleaning inside and out: carpets are dusted and sunned; curtains are taken down and washed; and new furniture might even be bought.

Everyone, rich or poor, shops for new clothes for themselves and for the less fortunate. Business people give gifts to their employees, hoping this generosity will bestow upon them good luck for future business.

Just before the New Year, in every household candles burn in each room, creating an atmosphere of joy. A special table is set aside, with a candle and mirror in the center. The Koran, a bowl of water with a floating leaf, fruit, and various colored items are also placed on the table. Family members gather to await the exact time signifying the New Year. The movement of the leaf on the water is a special sign that Iranians view as the start of the New Year. Quite often, in the larger cities and towns, a cannon is fired or a gong sounded to herald the New Year.

Now Ruz celebrations go on for 13 days; this is a period of socializing. Friends and relatives visit to wish one another happiness for the new year. Old quarrels are forgotten, and forgiveness is the main theme. Children enjoy this the most, perhaps, because they get money or other gifts. Older members of the household usually stay home during the first few days to welcome guests. They set the table with traditional homemade sweets and drinks, which they actively encourage their guests to try. Visitors arrive in a continuous stream from morning to evening.

The 13th day of the New Year is considered unlucky. In order to keep bad luck out of the house, the bowls of green shoots are thrown out, and most families go out for a picnic. An elaborate picnic lunch is packed, and everyone sets out by car or bus for some comfortable spot away from the home, hoping to chase away all the bad luck for the day.

During the 13-day New Year period, visits, gifts, and greetings are exchanged, and mounds of sweets eaten.

ASHURA

The 10th day of the month of Muharram is Ashura, the anniversary of the martyrdom of the Prophet's grandson Hussein in A.D. 680 at Karbala, a city in present-day Iraq. Although Muslims all over the world mourn his death, Shi'a Muslims consider the murder of Hussein by the army of the Umayyad caliph Yazid I a particularly dreadful crime. Thus Shi'a Muslims mourn Hussein's death in a public show of sorrow that lasts a whole month.

During the observance of Muharram, mourners make a procession through the streets and give themselves over to frenzied expressions of grief, flogging themselves with flails, cutting their bodies with blades, or piercing their skin with hooks. Sermons given at public places and at mosques reinforce the Prophet's teachings and highlight stories about Hussein's sufferings.

Shi'a Muslims also mark the tragedy at Karbala with passion plays, or *ta'ziyeh* (tah-ZHIH-yah), usually acted out in three acts: the first act deals with events before the battle; the second deals with the battle itself; and the third deals with events following the battle.

To commemorate the tragic circumstances of the martyr's deaths, many well-to-do Iranians donate money and goods to the poor. Some hold feasts for the poor. There are no weddings or parties during Muharram, and red is forbidden. Some men wear black.

NATIONAL HOLIDAYS

Iran's national holidays celebrate major events in the nation's recent history. The holiday on February 11 celebrates the fall of Reza Shah. Oil Nationalization Day, on March 20, is the anniversary of Iran's assumption of control of its oil from the Western powers that had been profiting from it.

Then in March there is, of course, the Iranian New Year, called Now Ruz. This starts on the 21st, and although the holidays run until the 25th, visiting and feasting goes on for 13 days.

April 1 is not known as April Fool's Day in Iran; it is Islamic Republic Day. People come out into the streets in large numbers, carrying placards with life-size—or larger than life-size—pictures of their beloved leader, Ayatollah Khomeini. Western nations, seen as enemies of the revolution, are often targets of Iranian disapproval; this shows on placards carrying anti-Western slogans.

A street festival takes on a carnival atmosphere on a national holiday in Iran.

FOOD

FOOD, GLORIOUS FOOD! That is what Marco Polo probably thought when he sampled the famous melons of Persia. Iranians still grow an incredible variety of melons, and there are some street stalls that sell only melons. But apart from melons, Iranian food is often regarded as one of the most refined cuisines in the Middle East.

Today Iranian cuisine is particularly well-known for its rice dishes. Nowhere in the world—except perhaps in India—do people give so much time and care to the preparation of rice dishes.

Bread is another favorite food in Iran. There is an amazing variety of unleavened breads to choose from every morning.

Authentic traditional Iranian cuisine is very old. It was born in the early days of the first Persian empire. It has since grown in sophistication. External influences have, of course, affected the development of Iranian cuisine. Some areas in the south of the country serve curries, an influence from India, while the Arab influence is more evident in areas around the Persian Gulf. Turkish influence is strong near the border with Turkey and Azerbaijan.

The home is the heart of Iranian cuisine. Every homemaker has her own unique and imaginative cooking style, based on secrets that she has inherited from her mother or grandmother.

Side dishes are an essential part of Iranian cuisine; strictly speaking, Iranians do not categorize dishes as entrées and main courses. The main course of rice or bread is extended to include a wide range of side dishes, depending on the number of people sharing the meal.

Above: **Radishes and spring onions at a stall in a bazaar.**

Opposite: **Spice sellers at a bazaar stand ready to weigh customers' orders.**

A vegetable vendor sells his produce off the back of a donkey.

MEAT AND FISH

Muslim Iranians do not eat pork, because Islam forbids it. They do not eat much beef either, because the country lacks large enough grazing lands to support sizeable herds of cattle.

Lamb is the favorite meat in Iran, often slaughtered when only a few days old. In the desert, lamb is slaughtered just before a meal, then spit-roasted over an outdoor fire. For roasting, lamb is usually stuffed with a mixture of rice, almonds, currants, and pine nuts.

One of the most popular dishes in Iran is *chelo kebab* (CHEH-loh KEE-bahb). Tender boneless lamb is the traditional meat used for the kebab. Pieces of meat and vegetables are spiked on metal skewers. The meat is usually marinated in a spice-laced yogurt mixture before being cooked.

The kebabs are grilled over hot coals and served on a bed of rice with side dishes of raw onions and cucumber. Marinated chicken on a skewer is called *jujeh kebab* (jew-JEH KEE-bahb).

Fish, such as trout and sturgeon, is a very popular food among Iranians in the Caspian area. Iranian fishers have many stories about catching sturgeon. They claim that sturgeon can live to be a century old and can weigh over a ton.

Sturgeon roe, or caviar, is a delicacy; it is too expensive for most Iranians, and much of it is exported.

A lot of meat consumed by Iranians comes from sheep.

PERSIAN INFLUENCE ON INDIAN CUISINE

When the Moghuls invaded India and established their empire, they brought not only the religion of Islam but also introduced the much-admired cuisine of Persia to northern India. Mughulai cuisine is well-known for its style of presentation. Mountains of rice streaked with saffron and garnished with nuts, raisins, and silver leaf accompany meat dishes cooked in rich smooth sauces. *Kurmah* (KOR-mah), *kofta* (KOF-tah), *briani* (bree-AH-ni), and *pilau* (POO-lau) are common dishes in both Iranian and northern Indian cuisine.

Fresh *naan* ready to go into a traditional oven.

RICE AND BREADS

Rice is the most important component of the daily diet of most Iranians. Rice is relatively cheap as it is largely grown locally, mostly on the Caspian coast. A typical meal consists of a mountain of cooked rice and small servings of vegetables, meat, or fish.

An Iranian national rice dish is *chelo* (CHEH-loh). This is plain rice, boiled and buttered. When served with a special sauce, it is called *chelo khoresh* (CHEH-loh KOO-resh). The sauce is a subtle blend of vegetables and meats, sweetened or soured by the juices of pomegranates, apples, quinces, and unripe grapes.

Polo (POH-loh) is another Iranian national rice dish; it is also known as *pilau* in the rest of the Middle East and in northern India. *Polo* is aromatic rice cooked with several ingredients that could include any combination of vegetables, fruit, nuts, and meats.

Although rice is still popular in Iran, the government is encouraging people to eat more bread instead, because wheat cultivation does not consume as much water as rice cultivation does. The government thus gives wheat farmers subsidies, making bread more affordable.

Bread shops in Iran are usually small, with a simple griddle to cook bread or an oven to bake it. Iranian breads come in different shapes and sizes. There is the coarse bread called *sanggak* (sahn-GAHK), made of wholemeal flour and baked over hot stones; *naan* (nahn) is an oval-shaped pancake-like bread that is either ovenbaked or cooked over a bed of small stones (*naan sanggak* is "dimpled"). The bread seller usually delivers the different types of bread on a specially adapted bicycle, motorcycle, or van. Bakeries stack *naan* in piles. Iranian bread is often sold by weight.

SIDE DISHES AND SOUPS

Vegetable side dishes vary from region to region in Iran; eggplant and spinach are very popular in most parts. Raw onions and shallots are often served with rice dishes. Stuffed vegetables called *dolmeh* (DOHL-meh) are convenient finger foods that can be taken to a picnic. Eggs are a versatile side dish; they are usually beaten together with finely chopped vegetables and herbs and made into a thick omelette that is cut into small enough pieces for the fingers to manage.

Koftas are no ordinary meatballs. They are usually made from finely minced mutton or lamb, heavily spiced with herbs and stuffed with fried onions, currants, chopped nuts, and often a boiled egg in the center.

Soups are very popular in Iran. Sometimes they are served as a meal; a worker would be satisfied with *abgoosht* (up-GOOSHT), a hearty mutton soup thickened with chickpeas. Chickpeas themselves make a side dish for bread or rice dishes. Chickpeas may be boiled after soaking in water for several hours or puréed with oil and used as a dip for breads.

127

IRANIAN DRINKS AND SWEETS

After a hearty meal, Iranians indulge in a wide range of fruit—quinces, pears, pomegranates, grapes, dates, apricots, peaches, and of course the famous Iranian melons. The fruits are usually offered sliced, sometimes sweetened with rose water, or crushed and served as a colorful sherbet.

People in Shiraz enjoy *palouden* (PAO-loo-den), a rose-flavored ice drink laced with lemon juice. Rose essence and rose water are used in many dishes. The essence is extracted from a variety of special roses. Of course, the ever-popular yogurt drink (yogurt whisked with water and mint) and tea are favorites during the hot months.

Iranians have a sweet tooth, but their desserts are not as sweet as those of many other Middle Eastern countries. Iranian sweets are usually made specially for festive occasions and holidays.

YOGURT—THE PERSIAN MILK

Yogurt was part of Iranian cusine fom the early days, when it was referred to as "Persian milk." Nearly all yogurt is homemade, and it is used widely in cooking and for general consumption. It has found its way into Iranian life in many guises, and Iranians consider it a miracle food. Here are several reasons why:

Yogurt can be used to make many kinds of dishes and drinks. It is added to cold and hot soups. It is used in salads. And sometimes it is whisked with water and mint to make a wonderfully cool thirst quencher on summer days.

Yogurt contains an enzyme that helps to break down meat tissues, tenderizing the meat in the process. It also helps spices to penetrate deep into the meat, thus enhancing the flavor of the meat.

Iranian yogurt is usually thick-set and tastes rich and creamy. It is made from whole milk. If the fat is extracted, as in non-fat yogurt, it becomes too watery.

Iranians claim that yogurt can cure ulcers, relieve sunburn, and even prolong one's life. Some people use yogurt as a face mask.

A fruit market in a bazaar.

Halva (HAHL-wah) and *baklava* (bahk-LAH-vah) are common throughout the Middle East and very popular in Iran. The Iranian variety of *baklava* is smaller and not as sweet. *Halva* is made of flour, shortening, sugar, and nuts.

Nuts, raisins, and preserved fruits are popular snack foods for Iranians looking for something to nibble on between meals or with a glass of strong Iranian tea.

SALMON KEBAB

This recipe serves four.

1½ pounds (680 g) salmon steak, washed
1 medium onion, grated
½ cup + 1½ tablespoons lemon juice
A little black pepper

1 teaspoon melted unsalted butter
1 teaspoon tomato paste
¼ cucumber, sliced thickly
1 medium tomato, sliced thickly

Cut the salmon into thick slices. In a bowl, toss the salmon with the grated onion, ½ cup lemon juice, and a little pepper. Refrigerate overnight. In a pan, mix the butter, tomato paste, and remaining lemon juice. Boil to make the basting sauce, then set aside. Thread the salmon, cucumber, and tomato slices on metal skewers. Grill over hot charcoal for about five minutes, brushing the fish and vegetables with the sauce twice. Serve with rice.

PERSIAN BEEF-STUFFED APPLES

These beef-stuffed apples may be eaten on their own or with rice. This recipe serves six.

¼ cup yellow split peas
1 finely chopped onion
2½ tablespoons oil
1 pound (454 g) ground beef
Salt and black pepper to taste
½ teaspoon ground cinnamon

12 washed large apples
A little butter
2½ cups water
7 tablespoons wine vinegar
2 tablespoons sugar

Preheat oven to 375°F (190°C). Boil the peas until soft, and drain. Lightly fry the onion in oil. Add the beef, and fry gently until the meat changes color. Mix in the salt, pepper, cinnamon, and peas. Cut out enough from the center of the apples to make room for the filling. Discard the core; chop up the extra flesh, and spread in a large baking dish. Stuff the apples with the fried filling, and put them on the chopped apple in the dish. Put a bit of butter on each apple. Pour 2 cups water in the dish, and bake for about half an hour, or until the apples are slightly cooked. Add the vinegar and sugar to ½ cup water, and boil to make a syrup. Pour a little syrup into each apple, and bake for another 15 minutes, or until tender. (Do not bake too long, or the apples will become mushy and the skin will break.)

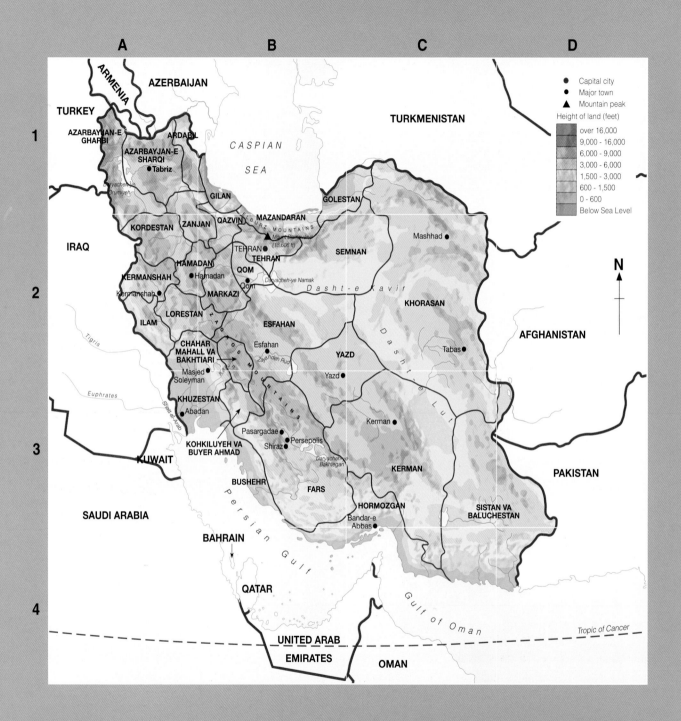

MAP OF IRAN

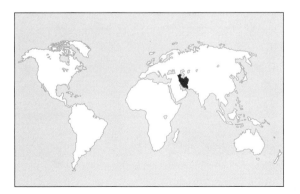

ECONOMIC IRAN

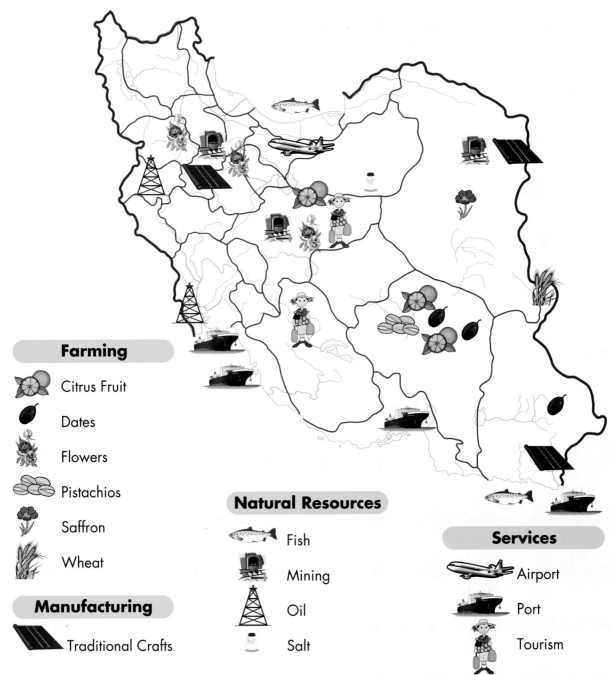

Farming

- Citrus Fruit
- Dates
- Flowers
- Pistachios
- Saffron
- Wheat

Manufacturing

- Traditional Crafts

Natural Resources

- Fish
- Mining
- Oil
- Salt

Services

- Airport
- Port
- Tourism

ABOUT THE ECONOMY

OVERVIEW

Iran is slowly reducing its dependence on oil-related products, and state-owned enterprises are being privatized. However, outdated machinery and practices hinder increases in agricultural production, and conservative leaders oppose measures to attract more foreign investment. Since 2002 fuel, energy, and food subsidies are being reduced, following a single exchange rate system. Despite U.S. sanctions, economic growth has been reasonably strong. Inflation has been steady, and unemployment is growing.

GROSS DOMESTIC PRODUCT (GDP)

US$426 billion (2001 estimate)

GDP SECTORS

Agriculture 20 percent, industry 24 percent, services 56 percent (2001 estimate)

WORKFORCE

17.3 million (1999 estimate)
Agriculture 30 percent, industry 25 percent, services 42 percent

CURRENCY

Iranian rial (IRR)
Notes: 100; 200; 500; 1,000; 2,000; 5,000; and 10,000 rial. Coins: 5, 10, 50, 100, 250 rial
USD 1 = IRR 8,117.75 (March 2003)

LAND AREA

631,663 square miles (1,636,000 square km)

LAND USE

Permanent pastures 27 percent, arable land 10 percent, permanent crops 1 percent, forests and woodland 7 percent, others 55 percent

AGRICULTURAL PRODUCTS

Wheat, rice, barley, corn, nuts, sugar beets, citrus fruit, dates, tea, dairy products, caviar, cotton, wool, hemp, flowers, tobacco

UNEMPLOYMENT RATE

16 percent (2002 estimate)

INFLATION RATE

11.4 percent (2002 estimate)

MAJOR EXPORTS

Petroleum, carpets, fruit, nuts, animal hides, iron and steel, chemicals, caviar

MAJOR IMPORTS

Industrial materials, machinery, consumer goods, food products, military supplies, pharmaceuticals

MAJOR TRADE PARTNERS

Italy, France, Germany, South Korea, United Arab Emirates, Japan, China

PORTS

Abadan, Anzali, Bandar-e Abbas, Bandar-e Imam Khomeini, Bushehr, Khorramshahr, Noshahr

CULTURAL IRAN

Beaches and caviar
Iran's Caspian coast is a beach holiday destination for tourists and Iranians alike. The eggs of mature Caspian sturgeon are used to make more than 80 percent of the world's caviar, known in the region as black gold.

Imam Reza Shrine
Iran's holiest city, Mashhad, is the center of a pilgrimage that attracts millions of Muslims from around the world every year. They come to visit the shrine of Imam Reza, the eighth Shi`a spiritual leader.

Trekking
There are several routes climbers can take up to the summit of Iran's tallest mountain, Darmavand, in the Elburz range. Darmavand's peak is covered with snow throughout the year.

Art museums
Iran's capital city, Tehran, is home to many museums showcasing pottery, glassware, jewelry, Persian carpets, and other kinds of fine art, ancient and contemporary.

Esfahan
Characterized by blue-tiled mosques, this city of architectural wonders, ancient bridges, and a great central square and bazaar inspired the saying "Esfahan is half the world."

Tomb of Cyrus the Great
Pasargadae was the capital of the Persian empire until the death of the empire's founder, Cyrus the Great. Cyrus' tomb was discovered at Pasargadae in 1951.

Shiraz
This beautiful garden city is famous for the rose of the same name. Home to the great Persian poets Hafiz and Sa`di, Shiraz is today a major center of learning.

Gate of All Nations
Persepolis was the capital of the Persian empire during the reign of Darius the Great, before the city was destroyed by Alexander the Great. The ruins at Persepolis include the Gate of All Nations and the Palace of 100 Columns.

ABOUT THE CULTURE

OFFICIAL NAME
Islamic Republic of Iran

CAPITAL
Tehran

GOVERNMENT
Theocratic republic

NATIONAL FLAG
The Iranian flag has three stripes—green on top, white in the middle, and red at the bottom. The green and red stripes are bordered with the slogan *Allab-o-Akbar* (AWL-lah-u-AHK-bar), which means "Allah is the greatest." The emblem of the Islamic republic is set in the center of the white stripe. It is in red and graphically represents the words "There is no god but Allah."

NATIONAL ANTHEM
Anthem of the Islamic Republic of Iran

POPULATION
66,622,704 (2002 estimate)
Growth rate 0.77 percent

LIFE EXPECTANCY
Total population 70 years; men 69 years, women 71 years (2002 estimate)

LITERACY RATE
72.1 percent

ETHNIC GROUPS
Persian 51 percent, Azeri 24 percent, Gilaki and Mazandarani 8 percent, Kurdish 7 percent, Arab 3 percent, Lur 2 percent, Baluchi 2 percent, Turkic 2 percent, other 1 percent

RELIGIOUS GROUPS
Shi'a Muslim, 89 percent; Sunni Muslim, 10 percent; Zoroastrian, Jewish, Christian, Baha'i, 1 percent

NATIONAL HOLIDAYS
Fall of the shah (February 11), Oil Nationalization Day (March 20), Now Ruz (March 21–25), Islamic Republic Day (April 1)

LEADERS IN POLITICS
Ayatollah Khamenei—chief of state
Muhammad Khatami—popularly elected president

LEADERS IN LITERATURE
Ferdowsi (940–1020)—poet who wrote the famous epic *Shahnameh*
Hafiz (1324–91)—poet
Omar Khayyam (1048–1123)—mathematician and poet who wrote the *Rubaiyat*

TIME
Greenwich Mean Time plus 3½ hours (GMT+0330); in summer plus 4½ hours (GMT+0430)

WORK HOURS AND DAYS
40-hour work week; about 30 days vacation

TIME LINE

IN IRAN	IN THE WORLD
2000 B.C. Central Asians migrate to Iran.	
	753 B.C. Rome is founded.
530–330 B.C. Cyrus the Great founds the Persian empire.	
330 B.C. Alexander the Great conquers Persia.	
323 B.C. Alexander dies; one of his generals forms the Seleucid dynasty.	
250 B.C. Parthian invaders establish their empire.	
	116–17 B.C. The Roman Empire reaches its greatest extent, under Emperor Trajan (98-17).
A.D. 224 The Sassanids found the second Persian empire.	
	A.D. 600 Height of Mayan civilization
A.D. 637 Arabs conquer Persia; Islam becomes the state religion.	
1051–1220 Reign of the Seljuks	**1000** The Chinese perfect gunpowder and begin to use it in warfare.
1258 Mongol invaders establish the Il-Khanid dynasty.	
1335 The Mongol dynasty falls apart; a succession of minor dynasties follows.	
1501–1722 The Safavids rule the third Persian empire.	
	1530 Beginning of trans-Atlantic slave trade organized by the Portuguese in Africa.
	1558–1603 Reign of Elizabeth I of England
	1620 Pilgrims sail the *Mayflower* to America.
	1776 U.S. Declaration of Independence
	1789–1799 The French Revolution

IN IRAN	IN THE WORLD
1796–1925 Reign of the Qajars	
	1861 The U.S. Civil War begins.
	1869 The Suez Canal is opened.
	1914 World War I begins.
1926 Reza Khan founds the Pahlavi Dynasty.	
1935 Persia is named Iran.	
1941 British and Soviet forces invade. Reza Khan abdicates in favor of his son.	**1939** World War II begins.
	1945 The United States drops atomic bombs on Hiroshima and Nagasaki.
	1949 The North Atlantic Treaty Organization (NATO) is formed.
	1957 The Russians launch Sputnik.
	1966–1969 The Chinese Cultural Revolution
1979 The Islamic Revolution; Ayatollah Khomeini comes to power.	
1980 Iran becomes an Islamic republic.	
1980–88 Iran-Iraq War	
1989 Ayatollah Khomeini dies.	**1986** Nuclear power disaster at Chernobyl in Ukraine
	1991 Break-up of the Soviet Union
1997 Muhammad Khatami is elected president.	**1997** Hong Kong is returned to China.
	2001 Terrorists crash planes in New York, Washington, D.C., and Pennsylvania.
	2003 War in Iraq

GLOSSARY

ayatollah (AH-yah-toh-lah)
Title given to pious and learned religious men at the top of the Islamic Shi'a hierarchy.

caliph
A successor of Prophet Muhammad.

chador (CHAH-dorh)
Traditional clothes worn by Iranian women in public; it covers the body from head to toe.

djuba (ZHOO-bah)
A water channel.

hajj
An annual pilgrimage Muslims all over the world make to Islam's holy city Mecca.

halal
Permitted for consumption by Islamic law.

hookah (HOO-kah)
A water, or hubble-bubble, pipe for smoking.

kafekhanna (KAH-FEEK-hah-nah)
A coffeehouse turned teahouse.

kamenchay (kah-men-CHAY)
A spike-fiddle.

madraseh (MAH-drah-sah)
A religious school.

majlis (MAHJ-liz)
An assembly of elected representatives.

muezzin
A mosque official who announces prayer times.

mullah (MOO-LAH)
A Muslim teacher or scholar.

namak (NAH-mahk)
A shallow salt lake.

nay (NAY)
A traditional Iranian flute.

qanat (kah-NUT)
An underground water tunnel.

samovar
A metal urn for boiling tea.

santur (san-TOOR)
A traditional Iranian 72-string musical instrument.

shah
A sovereign, or king, of Iran.

Sufi (SOO-fi)
A follower of Sufism, or Islamic mysticism.

Sunna (SOON-nah)
A guide to Islamic teaching and law that includes the sayings of the Prophet Mohammed and his answers to philosophical and legal questions.

vali-ye faqih (VAH-li-yee fah-kee)
The spiritual leader of Iran; the most powerful person in the country.

FURTHER INFORMATION

BOOKS

Batmanglij, Najmieh. *A Taste of Persia: An Introduction to Persian Cooking*. Washington, D.C.: Mage Publishers, 1999.

Canby, Sheila R. *The Golden Age of Persian Art, 1501–1722*. New York: Harry N. Abrams, 2000.

Dehghani, Yavar. *Farsi (Persian) Phrasebook: The Language of Iran*. California: Lonely Planet, 2001.

Dennis, Anthony J. (editor). *Letters to Khatami: A Reply to the Iranian President's Call For a Dialogue Among Civilizations*. Indiana: Wyndham Hall Press, 2001.

Hofmeyr, Dianne and Jude Daly (illustrator). *The Stone: A Persian Legend of the Magi*. New York: Farrar, Straus, and Giroux, 1998.

O'Shea, Maria. *Culture Shock! Iran*. (Revised.) Oregon: Graphic Arts Center Publishing Company, 2003.

Schimmel, Annemarie (translator). *Look! This is Love: Poems of Rumi*. (Reissue). Boston: Shambhala Publications, 1996.

Yale, Pat, et al. *Lonely Planet Iran*. (3rd ed.) California: Lonely Planet, 2001.

WEBSITES

Central Intelligence Agency World Factbook (select Iran from the country list). www.cia.gov/cia/publications/factbook

Embassy of The Islamic Republic of Iran in Ottawa, Canada. www.salamiran.org

Green Party of Iran. www.iran-e-sabz.org/eindex.html

Human Rights Watch (type "Iran" in the search box). www.hrw.org

Intercaspian Photo Bank. www.intercaspian.com

Lonely Planet World Guide: Destination Iran. www.lonelyplanet.com/destinations/middle_east/iran

NetIran. www.netiran.com

Payvand: Iran News, Directory, and Bazaar. www.payvand.com

Statistical Center of Iran. www.sci.or.ir

FILM

Kiarostami, Abbas (director). *Taste of Cherry*. Home Vision Entertainment, 1998. (DVD)

Majidi, Majid (director). *Children of Heaven*. Miramax, 1999. (DVD)

Panahi, Jafar (director). *The White Balloon*. Hallmark Home Entertainment, 1995. (VHS)

MUSIC

Persian Classical Music. Nonesuch, 1991. (CD)

Without You: Masters of Persian Music. World Village, 2002. (CD)

BIBLIOGRAPHY

Baker, Patricia. *Iran*. Bucks, United Kingdom: Bradt Travel Guides, 2001.

Dodwell, Christina. *A Traveller on Horseback: In Eastern Turkey and Iran*. New York: Walker, 1989.

Fox, Mary Virginia. *Iran*. Chicago: Children's Press, 1991.

Hole, Pat, Anthony Ham, and Paul Greenway. *Iran*. (3rd ed.) California: Lonely Planet, 2001.

Mackey, Sandra. *The Iranians*. London: Penguin, 1996.

Metz, Helen Chapin (editor). *Iran: A Country Study*. Washington: U.S. Government Printing Office, 1989.

Sanders, Renfield. *Iran*. New York: Chelsea House, 1990.

Wright, Martin (editor). *Iran: The Khomeini Revolution*. Countries in Crisis series. New York: Longman, 1989.

Iran in Pictures. Minneapolis: Lerner Publications, 1989.

INDEX